Cambridge Primary

Computing

Learner's Book 5

Roland Birbal
Carissa Gookool
Michelle Koon Koon
Shiva J. Maharaj
Nazreen Mohammed
Michele Taylor

Series editor:
Roland Birbal

Boost

HODDER
EDUCATION
AN HACHETTE UK COMPANY

Endorsement indicates that a resource has passed Cambridge International's rigorous quality-assurance process and is suitable to support the delivery of a Cambridge International curriculum framework. However, endorsed resources are not the only suitable materials available to support teaching and learning, and are not essential to be used to achieve the qualification. Resource lists found on the Cambridge International website will include this resource and other endorsed resources.

Any example answers to questions taken from past question papers, practice questions, accompanying marks and mark schemes included in this resource have been written by the authors and are for guidance only. They do not replicate examination papers. In examinations the way marks are awarded may be different. Any references to assessment and/or assessment preparation are the publisher's interpretation of the curriculum framework requirements. Examiners will not use endorsed resources as a source of material for any assessment set by Cambridge International.

While the publishers have made every attempt to ensure that advice on the qualification and its assessment is accurate, the official curriculum framework, specimen assessment materials and any associated assessment guidance materials produced by the awarding body are the only authoritative source of information and should always be referred to for definitive guidance. Cambridge International recommends that teachers consider using a range of teaching and learning resources based on their own professional judgement of their students' needs.

Cambridge International has not paid for the production of this resource, nor does Cambridge International receive any royalties from its sale. For more information about the endorsement process, please visit www.cambridgeinternational.org/endorsed-resources

Cambridge International copyright material in this publication is reproduced under licence and remains the intellectual property of Cambridge Assessment International Education.

Registered Cambridge International Schools benefit from high-quality programmes, assessments and a wide range of support so that teachers can effectively deliver Cambridge Primary. Visit www.cambridgeinternational.org/primary to find out more.

Third-party websites and resources referred to in this publication have not been endorsed by Cambridge Assessment International Education.

Although every effort has been made to ensure that website addresses are correct at time of going to press, Hodder Education cannot be held responsible for the content of any website mentioned in this book. It is sometimes possible to find a relocated web page by typing in the address of the home page for a website in the URL window of your browser.

Hachette UK's policy is to use papers that are natural, renewable and recyclable products and made from wood grown in well-managed forests and other controlled sources. The logging and manufacturing processes are expected to conform to the environmental regulations of the country of origin.

Orders: please contact Hachette UK Distribution, Hely Hutchinson Centre, Milton Road, Didcot, Oxfordshire, OX11 7HH. Telephone: +44 (0)1235 827827. Email education@hachette.co.uk. Lines are open from 9 a.m. to 5 p.m., Monday to Saturday, with a 24-hour message-answering service. You can also order through our website: www.hoddereducation.com

© Roland Birbal, Carissa Gookool, Michelle Koon Koon, Nazreen Mohammed, Michele Taylor 2023

First published in 2023 by
Hodder Education
An Hachette UK Company
Carmelite House
50 Victoria Embankment
London EC4Y 0DZ

www.hoddereducation.com

Impression number   10 9 8 7 6 5 4 3 2 1
Year   2027 2026 2025 2024 2023

Cover illustration by Lisa Hunt from the Bright Agency
Illustrations by Vian Oelofsen, Stéphan Theron
Typeset in FS Albert 12/14 by IO Publishing CC
Produced by DZS Grafik, Printed in Slovenia
A catalogue record for this title is available from the British Library.
ISBN 9781398368606

MIX
Paper | Supporting responsible forestry
FSC™ C104740

Contents

How to use this book

Get started! Talk about the new topic with a partner or small group.

You will learn: A list of things you will learn in the unit.

You will learn to:

- use variables in algorithms
- create a clear name for each variable
- develop programs with a variable
- write an outline plan for a program.

In this unit, you will develop algorithms and programs with variables using Scratch.

Warm up

Work in pairs. Look at the series of images for a story below.

A   B   C

D   E   F

Warm up: An offline activity to start your learning.

Re-arrange the images in the correct sequence to tell a story that makes sense.

1 Image __
2 Image __
3 Image __
4 Image __
5 Image __
6 Image __

Compare your answer with your partner's.

Do you remember?

Before you start this unit, check that you:

- know how to develop algorithms where two objects interrelate
- know how to develop programs where two or more objects can interact.

In this unit, you will use Scratch.
There is an online chapter all about Scratch.

Do you remember? A list of things you should know before you start the unit.

Learn

A **statistical investigation** happens when we need to solve a problem or answer a question that requires data.

Here are some examples of statistical investigations:

- You are asked to find out the three favourite fruits among students at your school. To do this, you need statistical data.
- You are given a project to see how light affects the growth of a plant. To do this, you need data.

When conducting a statistical investigation, the following steps must be taken:

Step 1: Plan how to collect the data.

Step 2: Collect the data.

Step 3: Carefully look at the data in many forms.

Step 4: Try to understand the data.

Step 5: Come to a conclusion.

Think about how you would collect data to find the answers to the two problems above.

We can use computing tools to help us in a statistical investigation. They include:

- data loggers
- databases
- spreadsheets
- document production software.

Data loggers

Data loggers are devices that collect data over a period of time. They are used for monitoring a process.

These devices have sensors that can collect data such as temperature, humidity, sound and pressure.

Data loggers collect data at regular times, known as intervals.

Here is a data logger to monitor the temperature.

Spreadsheets

Spreadsheet software is used to store, organise and represent data.

Data can be shown in the form of a table, graph or chart.

Spreadsheets are also used to:

- perform calculations on data
- sort data.

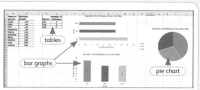

tables

bar graphs

pie chart

Learn: Learn new computing skills with your teacher. Look at the instructions to help you.

Practise

1. To do research, the following steps must be taken. Write these steps in the correct order in your notebook.

   A Try to understand the data

   B Collect the data

   C Come to a conclusion

   D Carefully look at the data in various forms

   E Plan how to collect the data

2. Here are some computing tools that can be used to collect, store and present data in different ways. State whether each of the computing tools is hardware or software.

   a Spreadsheets

   b Databases

   c Data loggers

   d Microsoft Word

3. This is a picture of a data logger.

   a Discuss with your partner what a data logger is.

   b Give some examples of the types of data a data logger can collect.

4. Match the computing tool with the correct description. Write the answers in your notebook.

Spreadsheets	Data is organised in a structured way
Data loggers	Can easily create charts from a data
Databases	Can be used to create a questionnaire
Google Docs	Collects data at regular intervals

5. a List three computing tools that can be used when carrying out a data study.

   b Explain the purpose of each computing tool listed in question **5a**.

Practise: Answer questions to learn more and practise your new skills.

How to use this book

Go further: Activities to make you think carefully about computing.

Go further

1 Write an algorithm for the **Pico** Sprite in a program:

- **Pico** should jump when the space key is pressed by a change in y by 50, then wait 0.2 seconds and then have a change in y by −50.
- The program should count every time the **Pico** Sprite jumps.
- The variable should add one (1) to itself every time a jump happens.
- The program should start counting from 0 (the variable should start at 0).

Part 1	
❶	Start program when …
❷	
❸	

Part 2	
❶	Start program when …
❷	
❸	
❹	
❺	

2 Give two reasons why variables should have a clear name.
3 Create the program in Scratch for the algorithm in part **1**.
- Search and select the **Pico** Sprite
- Add the **Colorful City** Backdrop.
4 Test your code and check that you get the correct results.

Challenge yourself!

Make changes to your program from the **Go Further** activity.

The **Text to Speech** extension blocks read text out loud.

1 Click the **Add Extension** button and add the **Text to Speech** Group to the Blocks Palette.
2 Add the code on the right to the Pico Sprite.
3 Add code to match the algorithm in the table to the **Giga Walking** Sprite.

Step	Instruction
❶	Start program when this sprite is clicked
❷	Switch to School Backdrop
❸	Set voice to squeak
❹	Speak "Yeah"

4 Add a third character to your program, the **Tera** Sprite. This sprite should give the results in the table.

Step	Instruction
❶	Start program when the Green Flag is clicked
❷	Switch to next costume
❸	Wait 3 seconds
❹	Hide

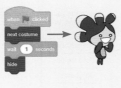

5 Debug the created code above to match the algorithm in the table and add the corrected code to the **Tera** Sprite.
6 Run your program and check that you get the required results.

Challenge yourself! A harder activity to test your new skills.

All links to additional resources can be found at: https://www.hoddereducation.co.uk/cambridgeextras

My project

Work in groups to complete the project. Write the answers in your notebook.

1 Imagine that you and your classmates are doing a science experiment to see how the humidity changes in a day.
   a State ONE computing tool that can be used to collect the data.
   b State ONE computing tool that can be used to represent the data as a chart.

2 The following data was collected.

Time	Humidity
9.00 a.m.	55.3
11.00 a.m.	54.0
1.00 p.m.	50.4
3.00 p.m.	47.1

   a What type of data is seen in the table?
   b What chart will be best suited to represent the data in the table?

3 Your teacher would like to know the most popular shoe colour in class.
   a What data should be collected to answer the question?
   b What question should she ask each student?
   c What are some ways of collecting the data from the students in your class?
   d What type of data will be collected: categorical, discrete or continuous?
   e After the data is collected, your teacher would like to see a sorted list of the students grouped by the colour of shoes. What is the best way to represent the data?
     • chart   • table
   f Choose the best chart to show the percentage of students with each colour of shoes.
     • line   • pie

My project: A longer activity at the end of the unit to test the skills you have learnt so far.

Did you know?

The first computer to use the binary code was the Z3 invented by Konrad Zuse in 1941.

Did you know? Learn about interesting facts and information.

What can you do? Find out how much you have learnt and what you can do.

What can you do?

Read and review what you can do.
✔ I can list computing tools that may be used during a statistical investigation.
✔ I can identify different ways of representing data.
✔ I know how to represent data to suit different criteria.
✔ I know how to collect data to answer questions.

Well done! You now know about various computing tools, how to present data and how to collect data to answer questions!

Computational thinking

Write an algorithm with a variable that displays the user's name: It should:
• Ask the user for their name.
• Store that answer as a variable called **Name**.
• Displays the word "Hello" and the value stored in the variable.

The output of your algorithm, for example, should say, "Hello Jack".

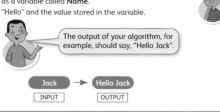

Jack → Hello Jack
INPUT   OUTPUT

Keywords

outcome: the result or way something turns out
event: a thing that happens or takes place
subprogram: a small program that is part of the main program.

Keywords: Understand new computing words. The **Glossary** at the end of the book also lists all of these words.

Computational thinking: A task that tests your computational thinking skills.

Unit 1 — Be a designer

Designing code with objects

Get started!

Have you ever played a game that needs two people? Work with your partner to make a list of games that need two or more people to play.

Does playing with another person make the game more fun and exciting?

You will learn to:

- develop algorithms where two objects interrelate
- develop programs where two or more objects can interact
- outline the skills of the different people needed to create a program.

In this unit, you will develop algorithms and programs with two or more objects.

Warm up

Work in groups of four. You will play a game that involves four players.

The object of the game is to reach the middle block first. Each player gets into position on one corner of the board below.

Each player can:

- only move one block at a time
- can block the move of another player by placing an X on one of the blocks.

Which player won?

How many blocks did the player take to win?

Do you remember?

Before you start this unit, check that you:

- can follow, understand, edit and correct an algorithm that uses repetition
- know how to develop programs with repetition
- can test different parts of a program to identify and debug errors.

Algorithms with two objects

In this section, we will develop an algorithm where one sprite character follows another sprite. Let's write the algorithm for the first sprite to move from one end of the screen to the other.

Algorithm Name: Chasing Game Penguin	
Step	**Instruction**
❶	When the Green Flag is clicked
❷	Set size to 50 %
❸	Glide 2 seconds to random position
❹	Repeat step 3 nine more times
❺	Stop program

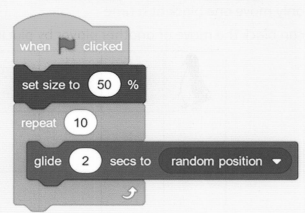

To create and run this program in Scratch:

1   Open a new project.

2   Choose any sprite for Sprite 1 and add the following code.

3   Add the **set rotation style left-right** block from the Motions group.

4   Select the **Repeat** block from the Control group.

5   Add the **Move ( ) steps** from the Motions group.

6   Add the **if on edge**, **bounce** block from the motions block.

We will now write an algorithm for the second sprite.

Algorithm Name: Chasing Game Polar Bear	
Step	**Instruction**
❶	When the Green Flag is clicked
❷	Point towards Penguin
❸	Glide 1 second to Penguin
❹	Repeat steps 2 and 3 nineteen more times
❺	Stop program

The **Polar bear** will now follow the **Penguin**, wherever it goes!

The **point towards** and **glide towards** blocks are in the **Motions** group. Once the **Penguin** sprite has been added to the program, it appears as an option in the drop-down menu in each block.

Practise

1   Complete the following algorithm for a third sprite in the chasing game. The **Dinosaur** sprite should chase the **Polar bear**.

Algorithm Name: Chasing Game Dinosaur	
Step	**Instruction**
❶	When the _____ is clicked
❷	Set size to 50 %
❸	Point towards _____
❹	Glide 0.5 seconds to _____
❺	Repeat steps ___ and ___ thirty nine more times
❻	Stop program

2   Create the code for this algorithm.

3   Run and test your code. Does the **Dinosaur** chase the **Polar bear**?

Algorithms and code with two objects

Learn

In this section, we will develop algorithms where one sprite talks to another sprite. When two sprites interact, we must write an algorithm for each sprite.

In the following algorithms, a **Fish** sprite will ask the **Dani** sprite's name three times. **Dani** will respond with a new name every time it is asked.

In the **Fish Sprite broadcast** algorithm, the **Fish** sends out a message (broadcasts) and waits to receive a response.

The code for this algorithm is:

Algorithm Name: Fish Sprite broadcast	
Step	**Instruction**
1	When the Green Flag is clicked
2	Say **What's your name?** for 2 seconds
3	Broadcast message 1 for 2 seconds
4	Say **What's your name?** for 2 seconds
5	Broadcast message 2 for 2 seconds
6	Say **What's your name?** for 2 seconds
7	Broadcast message 3 for 2 seconds
8	Stop program

The **Dani** sprite performs an action when it receives a message. In this case, the action for each message is different. This means we will write different algorithms for each message.

In the algorithm below, the **Dani** sprite says its name when it receives the first message. The **Dani** sprite then waits for a response from the **Fish** sprite.

The code for this algorithm is:

Algorithm Name: Dani Responds Costume 1	
Step	**Instruction**
1	When I receive broadcast **message 1**
2	Say **Hello! My name is Dani-a** for 2 seconds
3	Wait 2 seconds
4	Stop program

Did you know?

The **broadcast message** sends a message to all sprites.

The **broadcast message and wait** block waits for the sprite to respond to the instructions.

The **when I receive message** block tells a sprite what to do when they receive the message.

Practise

1   Fill in the algorithm for **Dani's** response to the second message. **Dani** should say that they are called **Dani-b**.

Algorithm Name: Dani Responds Costume 2	
Step	**Instruction**
❶	When I receive broadcast _____
❷	Say _____ for _____ seconds
❸	Wait _____ seconds
❹	Stop program

2   Write the algorithm for the third costume for **Dani's** response to the third message.

3   If you haven't already, create the code for the **Fish Sprite broadcast** algorithm and the **Dani Responds Costume 1** algorithm.

4   Create the code for the **Dani Responds Costume 2** algorithm.

5   Create the code for the **Dani Responds Costume 3** algorithm.

The **broadcast message** block is in the **Events** group. You can select which message to broadcast, or create new messages, by clicking on the drop down.

Skills of the program team

Creating a final program needs a number of key people with different skills. These people work as part of a team to complete the final program.

The project manager

Anna is the project manager. She makes sure that everyone on the team gets their work done.

She assigns tasks, tells each member of the team what they have to do and ensures the task is done on time.

She is skilled in communication, planning and organising tasks.

The computer engineer

Chrissy is a computer engineer. She must understand how hardware works together with the software.

She is usually part of the team when software is written for specific hardware – for instance, a microwave.

The programmer

Kala is skilled in writing programs using different programming languages. She knows how to program in Scratch!

She writes the software for games and other programs.

The designer

Jarno is responsible for how a program looks and feels for the user.

If the program is a game, Jarno is the artist who designs the look of characters, background scenes and different levels.

The testers

Jim makes sure that the finished program does not have any bugs. He has to test the program systematically.

If he finds a bug, it means that the program is not doing what it was intended to do. Jim records the error, and sends it back to the programmer and designer to fix.

Practise

1 Which one of the following statements is true about a project manager?
   A They design how characters in a game look.
   B They are skilled in writing programs.
   C They ensure that the program has no bugs.
   D They are skilled in organising tasks.

2 Which of the following is NOT true about a project manager?
   A They are skilled in communicating with the members of the team.
   B They assign the task to each member of the team.
   C They ensure the tasks get done on time.
   D They are responsible for the look and feel of the software.

3 State whether the following are true or false:
   a Testers are optional when creating a final program.
   b Without a programmer, you cannot create the final program.
   c A programmer knows only one computer language.
   d A computer engineer knows how hardware functions with the software.

4 Work in groups of 3–4.
   You have been asked to recruit some students at your school onto your Program Team.
   Write a letter describing the different roles on your team and the skills that each role needs.

Go further

1 Copy and fill in the blanks using the word bank below.

captain | tester | project manager | programmer | computer engineer | designer

A _____ is responsible for how a program looks and feels. The _____ ensures that there are no bugs. The _____ is skilled in writing programs. The _____ _____ designs and builds the hardware components that works with the software. The _____ _____ is skilled in communication and is the team _____.

2 In Stage 4, you learnt how to add a sub-routine.

You wrote code for the **Chasing Game** in an earlier **Learn** panel.

a Write the Scratch code to match the **Jump Sub-routine** algorithm below. Add the code to the **Penguin**. This code will make the sprite jump.

Algorithm Name: Jump Sub-routine	
Step	**Instruction**
1	Define Jump Sub-routine
2	Change y by 40
3	Wait 1 second
4	Change y by −40

b Add a call to **Jump** sub-routine in the **Chasing Game Penguin** algorithm. The sub-routine should be called after the **Penguin** glides.

c Add the code for the sub-routine call to the **Chasing Game Penguin** code.

3 a Complete a second algorithm for the **Penguin** sprite to:
  - send message1 "**You can't catch me!**"
  - send message2 "**Who is behind you?**"

Algorithm Name: Jump Sub-routine	
Step	**Instruction**
1	When the Green Flag is clicked
2	Say _____ for 2 seconds
3	Broadcast _____ for 2 seconds
4	Say _____ for 2 seconds
5	Broadcast _____ for 2 seconds
6	Stop program

Challenge yourself!

You will create a new chasing game.

This game will contain three sprites: the **Fish**, the **Octopus** and the **Shark**.

The **Fish** should:

- Glide for 3 seconds towards the mouse pointer when the Green Flag is clicked
- Change to a random costume at the end of each glide
- This should repeat 8 times.

The **Octopus** should:

- Say "Are you coming?" for 1 second when the Green Flag is clicked
- Glide for 1 second towards the **Fish**
- Point towards the **Fish** at the end of the glide
- Broadcast a message at the end of each glide
- This should repeat 12 times.

The **Shark** should:

- Glide for 1 second towards the **Octopus** when it receives a message
- Say "I heard you!"
- Change costume at the end of the glide.

1 Write the algorithms for each sprite.

2 Write the code for each sprite.

3 Run and test your programs. Do the sprites behave as described?

My project

1   a   Conduct research to determine if there are any other people that can be added to a programming team.

    b   What skills should they have?

    c   Create a flyer to advertise the job position. Include the skills that this person must have on your flyer.

2   In the first **Learn** panel and **Practise** panel, we created an algorithm for up to three sprites to talk to each other. Create an algorithm where four sprites talk to each other. Convert the algorithm to code.

3   In this project, we will create a new Chasing Game. However, we will make it more complex by having the sprites record their position by drawing a circle.

    a   Add the **Pen extension** blocks to the palette.

    b   In the algorithm below, Sprite 1 moves randomly six times. Write the code to match this algorithm. (Hint: see **Learn** panel – Algorithm with two objects.) You can use any sprite.

Algorithm Name: Chasing Game Sprite 1 – Random position	
Step	**Instruction**
❶	When the Green Flag is clicked
❷	Set position to: x =125, y = 70
❸	Say "You can't catch me!" for 1 second
❹	Glide 2 seconds to random position
❺	Call Circle Sub-routine
❻	Repeat steps 3 to 6 five more times
❼	Stop program

    c   Below is the algorithm for the sub-routine to draw a circle. Write the code to match the Circle Sub-routine algorithm.

Algorithm Name: Circle Sub-routine	
Step	**Instruction**
❶	Define Circle sub-routine
❷	Set pen colour to 50
❸	Pen down
❹	Move 10 steps
❺	Turn right 36 degrees
❻	Repeat steps three and four 10 times
❼	Pen up

d   Add two additional Sprites into your Chasing Game project. You can choose any sprites.

The code for Sprite 2 and Sprite 3 is exactly the same as Sprite 1 except that:

- Sprite 2 should follow Sprite 1
- Sprite 3 should follow Sprite 2
- Different pen colours should be chosen.

Remember: A pen colour of 50 is blue. Different numbers are used for different colours.

e   Test your code and debug any errors.

What can you do?

Read and review what you can do.

Well done! You can now program sprites to interact with each other!

✔ I can develop algorithms where two objects interact.

✔ I can develop programs where more than two objects interrelate.

✔ I can state the skills of different persons required to create a program.

Representing data

Get started!

Here are two different ways to show the same data. Work with your partner to answer the questions.

A

Name	Age
Henry	9
Jasmine	10
Kent	9

B

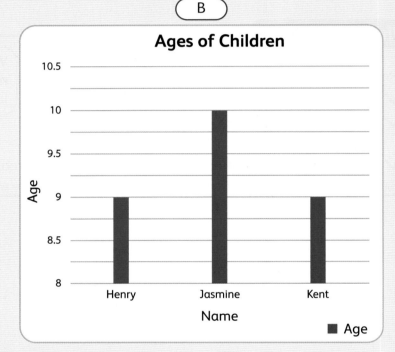

1   How is the data represented in A?

2   How is the data represented in B?

3   Which of the two is used to collect and organise the data?

4   Which of the two is used to present the data in graphical form?

You will learn:

- about computing tools that are used to collect data
- how to represent data in different ways
- how to represent data to suit different criteria
- how to collect data to answer questions.

In this unit, you will learn about computing tools for collecting, managing and representing data.

Warm up

Work with your partner. Match the data to be collected in the right column to answer the questions in the left column.

Question	Data to be collected
1 How many students have brown hair in the class?	a Number of badges each Scout earned
2 How many students are in the robotics club?	b Maths scores of students
3 Who earned the most badges in Scouts?	c Clubs that students are in
4 What is the highest maths score in class?	d Total number of each candy bought
5 Which is the most popular candy bought at the candy store?	e Hair colour of students

Do you remember?

Before you start this unit, check that you:
- know different ways of representing data using a digital tool
- know how to record data using computing devices
- know how to select data to solve problems.

Computing tools
Statistical investigations

Learn

A **statistical investigation** happens when we need to solve a problem or answer a question that requires data.

Here are some examples of statistical investigations:

- You are asked to find out the three favourite fruits among students at your school. To do this, you need statistical data.
- You are given a project to see how light affects the growth of a plant. To do this, you need data.

When conducting a statistical investigation, the following steps must be taken:

Step 1: Plan how to collect the data.

Step 2: Collect the data.

Step 3: Carefully look at the data in many forms.

Step 4: Try to understand the data.

Step 5: Come to a conclusion.

> Think about how you would collect data to find the answers to the two problems above.

We can use computing tools to help us in a statistical investigation. They include:

- data loggers
- databases
- spreadsheets
- document production software.

Data loggers

Data loggers are devices that collect data over a period of time. They are used for monitoring a process.

These devices have sensors that can collect data such as temperature, humidity, sound and pressure.

Data loggers collect data at regular times, known as **intervals**.

Here is a data logger to monitor the temperature.

Spreadsheets

Spreadsheet software is used to store, organise and represent data.

Data can be shown in the form of a table, graph or chart.

Spreadsheets are also used to:

- perform calculations on data
- sort data.

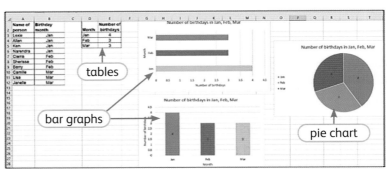

tables

bar graphs

pie chart

Databases

Database software stores data in a structured way. A database allows us to:

- enter data
- edit data
- search for data
- create reports from data.

Here is an example of a database that is used by a bakery. It allows the user to enter details about orders for cakes.

Cupcake Order Form

Office Use Only
OrderID   (New)

Initial   e.g. A
Surname   e.g. Amall

CupcakeFlavour   NumberOrdered
Please select from list provided: Vanilla, Chocolate, Lemon

DeliveryDate   e.g. 10/10/2022
Paid?

Document production tools

Document production software is used to create text-based documents. Some examples of document production software are Microsoft Word and Google Docs™.

They can be used to create documents such as questionnaires, forms and reports.

Pet Form

Pet's name:

Type of animal:

Reason for visit:

Temperature:

Shots: yes ☐   no ☐

Did you know?

Data loggers are used in many industries such as Food and Health. Data loggers save these industries millions of dollars daily by preventing waste.

Here is a data logger that is used to monitor the storage temperature of medication.

Keywords

statistical investigation: to carry out a study or research using data

interval: a given amount of time

Practise

1   To do research, the following steps must be taken.
    Write these steps in the correct order in
    your notebook.

    A   Try to understand the data

    B   Collect the data

    C   Come to a conclusion

    D   Carefully look at the data in various forms

    E   Plan how to collect the data

2   Here are some computing tools that can be used
    to collect, store and present data in different ways.
    State whether each of the computing tools is
    hardware or software.

    a   Spreadsheets

    b   Databases

    c   Data loggers

    d   Microsoft Word

3   This is a picture of a data logger.

    a   Discuss with your partner what a data
        logger is.

    b   Give some examples of the types of data a
        data logger can collect.

4   Match the computing tool with the correct
    description. Write the answers in your notebook.

Spreadsheets	Data is organised in a structured way
Data loggers	Can easily create charts from data
Databases	Can be used to create a questionnaire
Google Docs™	Collects data at regular intervals

5   a   List three computing tools that can be used when carrying out a data study.

    b   Explain the purpose of each computing tool listed in question **5a**.

Representing data
Discrete, categorical and continuous

There are three types of data that can be collected:

- discrete
- categorical
- continuous.

We learnt about discrete and categorical data in the previous unit.

Discrete data is whole numbers such as 1, 20 or 65. Discrete data is best represented as a bar or column chart.

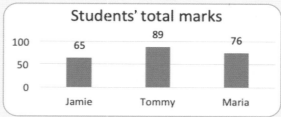

Categorical data is grouped into categories. The data may be represented as a pie, bar or column chart. This pie chart shows the number of people that bought a category of dessert.

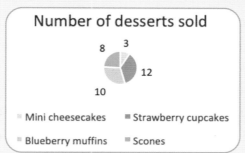

Continuous data does not have to be a whole number and can take any value. Continuous data is often used for things that can be measured.

For example, temperature can be measured and recorded as 35.0°C, 35.1°C, 35.2°C, 35.3°C, 35.4°C, 35.5°C, and so on.

Other examples of continuous data are height, time and amount of rainfall.

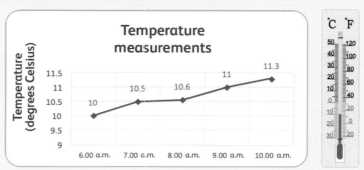

The best chart to represent data that is collected at regular points is a **line chart**.

In this example, the table shows the temperature collected every hour between 6 a.m. and 10 a.m. The **line chart** shows the temperature at each hour.

Time	Temperature (degrees Celsius)
6.00 a.m.	10.0
7.00 a.m.	10.5
8.00 a.m.	10.6
9.00 a.m.	11.0
10.00 a.m.	11.3

Using the chart, it is clear that there is a rise in temperature every hour.

It is easier to observe trends in data from a line chart.

Changing representations of data

There are times we may need to change how data is represented. This depends on what we want to do with the data. There are two main ways to represent data:

1   as a table

2   in graphical form – charts and graphs.

For example, we may want data values sorted in a particular order, or we may want to add data together. The best way to do this would be in a **table**.

The best chart to compare data values is a **column** or **bar chart**.

If we wish to show data values in the form of percentages, it is best to use a **pie chart**.

Spreadsheet software is a good tool for representing data as a table and as a **chart**.

Look at this table.

Customer	Ice-cream flavour	Orders
1	Vanilla	1
2	Chocolate	3
3	Chocolate	2
3	Strawberry	3
4	Strawberry	5

It shows the ice-cream orders of customers.

The owner of the ice-cream parlour would like to see the total orders of each type of ice cream.

The data can be represented as a **summary table**, as seen on the next page.

Ice-cream flavour	Orders
Vanilla	1
Chocolate	5
Strawberry	8

The owner also wants to see the ice-cream sales in graphical form, to compare the sales of each flavour. The data is selected from the summary table, and then the appropriate chart type is chosen in the spreadsheet.

It is easy to compare the sales in this chart. A bar or column chart is best suited to compare data.

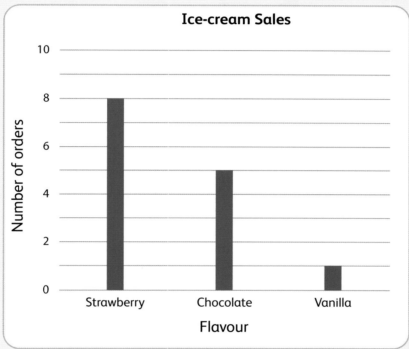

The owner also wants to see the percentage sales of each flavour in graphical form. He can choose the same data from the summary table, then select a pie chart.

Strawberry ice cream had the greatest percentage of sales – 57%.

A pie chart can show data as percentages. So, a pie chart is the best way to see the percentage sales.

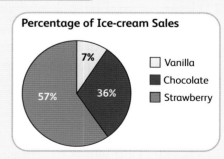

The same data was represented in three different ways.

Practise

Work in small groups to answer the following questions.

1 a What type of graph is shown?
- bar
- line
- pie

b What type of data is represented in the graph?
- discrete
- categorical
- continuous

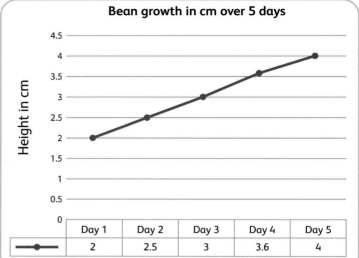

Bean growth in cm over 5 days

	Day 1	Day 2	Day 3	Day 4	Day 5
	2	2.5	3	3.6	4

2 a What type of graph(s) is best suited to represent categorical data?

b What type of graph(s) is best suited to represent discrete data?

Choose your answers from the options below. There may be more than one answer.

(bar)   (pie)   (line)   (column)

3 Mrs Hart collected the following data from her class.

Name of student	Test score
Damien Gilkes	78
Hannah Lee	85
Ramesh Singh	70
Bashir Karim	65

a Mrs Hart wants to see each student's test score from the highest to lowest. What is the best way to represent the data?
- line graph
- pie chart
- table

b Mrs Hart wants to represent the data in graphical form to compare test scores. What is the best way she can represent the data?
- line graph
- table
- column chart

Collecting data
To answer questions

Data can provide the answer to many questions. For example:

- Who got the highest mark in Science?
- What was the most popular snack sold this week?

To answer questions, we must first know what data is needed.

We can then work out the best way to collect the right data.

Look at the examples below to see how discrete and categorical data can be collected to answer a question.

Collecting data

Question 1: What is the most popular eye colour in class?

Data to be collected: There are 25 students in class, so data about the eye colour of all 25 students must be collected. The question to be asked is: "What is your eye colour?"

Remember, a good way to collect data from a large number of people is by using an electronic or paper-based form.

Ways of collecting the data: There are many ways of collecting data:

1. Observation – walk around the class, observe the eye colour of each student and record it.

2. Questionnaire – each student can answer a question about their eye colour on a form.

3. Interview – you could ask each student their eye colour and record their answer.

Type of data: The data to be collected is **categorical data**. The category options can be given in a form. This makes sorting data easy as it can be grouped by eye colour then counted.

What is your eye colour?				
Brown ❑	Blue ❑	Black ❑	Grey ❑	Green ❑

Question 2: How many children out of a group of 6 like the colour red?

Data to be collected: The response from 6 students. The question to be asked is: "Do you like the colour red?"

Ways of collecting the data: A small amount of data needs to be collected. The best way to collect this data is by asking each student and recording the answer (as seen in the table).

Type of data: The data to be collected is **categorical**. The response can be recorded under two categories, Yes and No. We can now easily count the number of students who like the colour red.

Student	Yes	No
Student1		
Student2		
Student3		
Student4		
Student5		
Student6		

Question 3: What is the average number of people in each house in Delhi?

Data to be collected: The number of people in each household. The question to be asked is, "How many people live in your house?"

Ways of collecting the data: Many people need to be asked this question. The best way to collect the data is by asking the question on a form.

Type of data: The data to be collected is **discrete**. This is because the answer can only be whole numbers. The number of people may be different in each home, so the question can be open-ended.

> **How many people live in your household?** _____

Practise

Work in groups to answer the questions.

1   The manager of the local supermarket wants to know the total number of times each customer visits the supermarket in a month.

   a   What data must be collected?
- Number of times each customer visits the supermarket in a month
- Number of times each customer drives to the supermarket.

   b   What type of data is collected?
     ❑ Discrete   ❑ Categorical

   c   What question should be asked of each customer?
- Where do you live?
- How many items do you buy in a month?
- How many times do you visit the supermarket in a month?

2   The manager wants to know the customer's favourite brand of milk. There are five different brands of milk.

   a   What data must be collected?
- Names of the five brands of milk
- Brand of milk each customer likes.

   b   What question should be asked of each customer?
- How many times do you buy milk?
- What is your favourite brand of milk?
- What is your favourite colour milk box?

> Refer to the **Learn** panel to help you with your answers.

   c   What type of data is collected?
     ❑ Discrete   ❑ Categorical

   d   The supermarket usually has hundreds of customers each day. The manager thinks the best way to collect the data is to stop each customer and ask them the question. Do you think this is the best way to collect the data? Why?

Go further

1   Complete the sentences with the correct words in the box.

(plan)   (look)   (understand)   (collect)   (conclusion)

To conduct an investigation, the following must be done:
a   ____ how to collect the data.   b   ____ the data.
c   Carefully ____ at the data in many forms.   d   Try to ____ the data.
e   Come to a ____.

2   Complete the questions.
a   What is a device used to collect data at regular intervals?
b   What kind of software is used to perform calculations and create charts?
c   What is an example of document production software?
d   What is the name of software that lets us store data in a structured way?

3   The weather station wants to track the amount of rainfall over 5 days.
a   The following data was collected: 2.5 mm, 1.5 mm, 2.2 mm, 2.3 mm, 1.7 mm.
    What type of data is this?
    •   discrete   •   categorical   •   continuous
b   What chart can best show the amount of rainfall over 5 days?
    •   pie chart   •   line chart   •   column chart

4   The data in the table shows how each student gets to school.
a   The teacher would like to see a list of the total number of students using each type of
    transportation. What is the best way to represent the data?
    •   summary table   •   pie chart   •   line chart
b   The principal would like to see the percentage of students who travel by car and bus in
    graphical form. What type of chart is best suited to represent the data?
    •   pie chart   •   line chart

5   Look at the following questions and discuss them with a classmate.

    Question: Which swim team earned the highest score amongst 10 teams at the
    Swimming Competition?
a   What data must be collected to answer the question?
    •   The names of the teams   •   The scores of the teams
b   What question should we ask each team?
    •   What is the name of your team?   •   What is your score?
    •   How many swimmers are in your team?
c   What type of data is collected, discrete or categorical?
d   To collect the data, we can walk around, ask each team their score and record it. Is this
    the best way to collect the data? Why?

Challenge yourself!

Work in pairs.

1 State whether the following is true or false:

   a Data loggers are devices that collect data over a period of time.

   b Microsoft Word is an example of spreadsheet software.

   c It is difficult to search for data in a database.

   d Charts can be created using spreadsheet software.

2 The Science class wants to see how salt affects the boiling point of water.

   a What type of graph is seen here?

   b What type of data is represented in this graph: discrete, categorical or continuous?

   c State the name of another chart that can be used to represent this type of data.

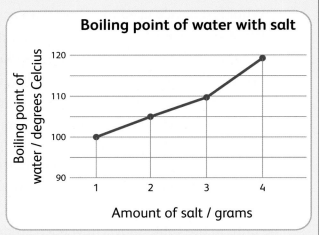

Boiling point of water with salt

3 a Here is a table with information about a club.

Club name	Number of members
Reading	10
Poetry	25
Art	20

   What type of chart is best suited to compare the number of members in each club?

   • pie chart   • line chart   • column chart

   b Give a reason for your choice of chart in question **3a**.

4 Mrs John wants to know the average number of questions that a class of 15 students answered correctly in a test.

   a What data must she collect?

   • The questions that were on the test

   • The number of correct answers for each student.

   b What question should she ask?

   • What subject was the test on?

   • How many questions were answered correctly?

   c What type of data is collected: discrete or categorical?

   d What is the best way/s to collect the data from the students?

   • Questionnaire – use a form

   • Observation – look at the number of questions each person got correct

   • Interview – ask each student how many questions they got correct.

   Give a reason for your answer.

My project

Work in groups to complete the project. Write the answers in your notebook.

1 Imagine that you and your classmates are doing a science experiment to see how the humidity changes in a day.

   a State ONE computing tool that can be used to collect the data.

   b State ONE computing tool that can be used to represent the data as a chart.

2 The following data was collected.

Time	Humidity
9.00 a.m.	55.3
11.00 a.m.	54.0
1.00 p.m.	50.4
3.00 p.m.	47.1

   a What type of data is seen in the table?

   b What chart will be best suited to represent the data in the table?

3 Your teacher would like to know the most popular shoe colour in class.

   a What data should be collected to answer the question?

   b What question should she ask each student?

   c What are some ways of collecting the data from the students in your class?

   d What type of data will be collected: categorical, discrete or continuous?

   e After the data is collected, your teacher would like to see a sorted list of the students grouped by the colour of shoes. What is the best way to represent the data?

     • chart   • table

   f Choose the best chart to show the percentage of students with each colour of shoes.

     • line   • pie

What can you do?

Read and review what you can do.

✔ I can list computing tools that may be used during a statistical investigation.

✔ I can identify different ways of representing data.

✔ I know how to represent data to suit different criteria.

✔ I know how to collect data to answer questions.

Well done! You now know about various computing tools, how to present data and how to collect data to answer questions!

Storage space

Get started!

Storing things in a specific place helps us keep our belongings safe and easy to find. It also keeps our things organised.

Discuss the following questions with a partner:

- What items would you store in the storage spaces shown in the pictures below?
- Does the storage space affect the size and quantity of the items you can store?
- How do you think each storage space shown is used?

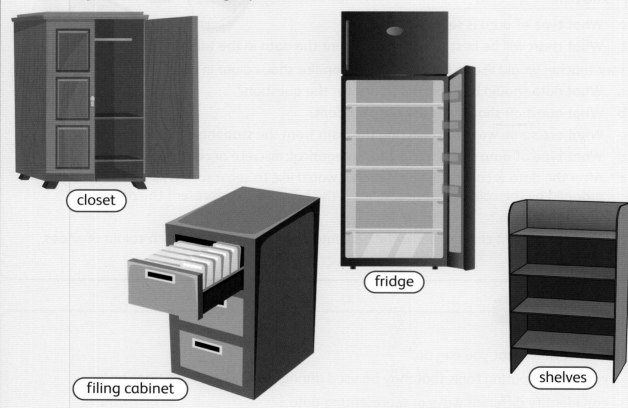

closet

filing cabinet

fridge

shelves

You will learn:

- that computers store data in binary
- about how we measure memory size
- about storage devices that can be used in computer systems.

In this unit, you will learn about how data is stored in a computer.

Warm up

Work in pairs.

- Seat your partner so that they cannot see the grid patterns below.
- Give your partner a blank 4 × 4 grid paper.
- Choose one of the grid patterns and describe it to your partner. A shaded square will be described as 'one' and a blank square will be 'zero'. You should describe one line at a time using only ones and zeros.
- Let your partner know when you start a new row and when you end a row.
- Your partner should shade a square when they hear 'one' and leave the square blank when they hear 'zero'.
- Once finished, compare your partner's drawing with the one you described.
- Switch places and try describing another grid pattern using ones and zeros.

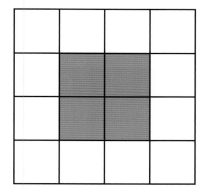

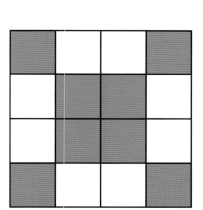

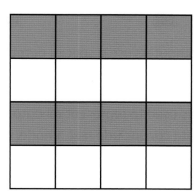

Do you remember?

Before you start this unit, check that you:

- know that different types of files can be stored on a computer's hard drive, including text, audio, image, video and games
- know these different types of files have different sizes.

Bits of storage

Learn

A computer is made up of many devices, including the **CPU**.

The CPU contains many tiny switches. Each switch can be **on** or **off**.

These switches are like a light bulb. A light bulb can only be **on** or **off**.

On and off can be represented by the numbers 1 and 0.

- 1 represents the state when the device is **on**
- 0 represents the state when the device is **off**.

There are billions of tiny switches in a modern computer!

Computers use a special number system to tell us whether their switches are on or off.

The **binary number system** consists of two digits: **1** and **0**.

It is used to represent all data stored in a computer.

Data can include text, image, audio, video and games.

ON	OFF
1	0

Every computer game you have ever played was made up of 1s and 0s!

Here is an example of how data is represented as binary.

Every character on the keyboard is stored as a different combination of zeroes and ones.

For example, when the uppercase letter **Z** on the keyboard is pressed, it sends an electrical signal to the computer. The computer converts that electrical signal to the binary code **0101 1010**.

The computer software displays the uppercase letter **Z** on the screen. However, the computer only sees the binary code **0101 1010**.

When the email is sent, the receiving computer only sees the binary code 0101 1010. When the software on that computer sees that binary code, it displays the uppercase **Z** on the screen.

Did you know?

The first computer to use the binary code was the Z3 invented by Konrad Zuse in 1941.

Keywords

CPU: a component that controls what a computer does

binary number system: a number system that contains two digits; 0 and 1

Practise

1 State whether the following statements are true or false:
   a A light bulb can be set to three positions.
   b Zero represents the state when the device is on.
   c The binary number system is used by computers to represent data.
   d Every character on a keyboard is represented by the same pattern of ones and zeros.

2 Copy the sentences and fill in the blanks using the words in the word bank below.

   (keyboard) (binary) (computer) (email) (electrical)

   If you are typing an _____ to a friend, when the uppercase letter 'Z' on the _____ is pressed, it sends an _____ signal to the _____, which is converted to the _____ code '0101 1010'.

3 Work with a partner to answer the following questions:
   a What is the binary number system?
   b Why is the binary number system used to represent data in a computer?

Units of storage

Learn

Bit

A **bit** is the smallest amount of data a computer can store.

It is short for binary digit and is represented by the numeral 0 or 1.

binary	**dig**its
bits	

Byte

One **byte** is made up of 8 bits.

One byte is used to represent a character on a keyboard. A character can be a letter, number, punctuation mark, symbol, or a blank space.

Each character has its own 8-bit binary code. All computers use the same code, called ASCII.

We have already seen the ASCII code for the uppercase Z.

Using ASCII codes, we can represent any word in binary.

For example, the word 'May' is converted to binary on the computer as follows:

- uppercase 'M' is 0100 1101
- lowercase 'a' is 0110 0001
- lowercase 'y' is 0111 1001.

Notice that the binary code for lowercase and uppercase letters on the ASCII binary character table is different.

ASCII Code – Character to Binary

0	0011 0000	I	0100 1001	a	0110 0001	t	0111 0100
1	0011 0001	J	0100 1010	b	0110 0010	u	0111 0101
2	0011 0010	K	0100 1011	c	0110 0011	v	0111 0110
3	0011 0011	L	0100 1100	d	0110 0100	w	0111 0111
4	0011 0100	M	0100 1101	e	0110 0101	x	0111 1000
5	0011 0101	N	0100 1110	f	0110 0110	y	0111 1001
6	0011 0110	O	0100 1111	g	0110 0111	z	0111 1010
7	0011 0111	P	0101 0000	h	0110 1000		
8	0011 1000	Q	0101 0001	i	0110 1001	:	0011 1010
9	0011 1001	R	0101 0010	j	0110 1010	;	0011 1011
		S	0101 0011	k	0110 1011	?	0011 1111
A	0100 0001	T	0101 0100	l	0110 1100	.	0010 1110
B	0100 0010	U	0101 0101	m	0110 1101	!	0010 0001
C	0100 0011	V	0101 0110	n	0110 1110	,	0010 1100
D	0100 0100	W	0101 0111	o	0110 1111	"	0010 0010
E	0100 0101	X	0101 1000	p	0111 0000	(	0010 1000
F	0100 0110	Y	0101 1001	q	0111 0001	)	0010 1001
G	0100 0111	Z	0101 1010	r	0111 0010	space	0010 0000
H	0100 1000			s	0111 0011		

Keywords

bit: smallest unit of storage in a computer.

byte: 1 byte is made up of 8 bits. The ASCII code for one character is 1 byte.

Storing larger files

We saw that the word 'May' is made of 3 bytes. If we wanted to store a whole sentence, we will need more bytes.

To store something useful on a computer system, you need a large number of bytes. We have special words to help us count these large numbers.

A kilobyte is equal to 1024 Bytes.

A kilobyte is enough space to store a short text document with about 1000 characters.

A low-quality picture would need about 100 kilobytes.

A megabyte is 1024 kilobytes.

With one megabyte you can store:

- about 1 minute of audio in MP3 format
- about 400 pages of a book.

A high-quality picture may need around 5 megabytes.

Small text document
1 Kilobyte

Low-quality photo
100 Kilobyte

Small text document
1 Kilobyte

High-quality photo
5 Megabytes

8 Bits	= 1 Byte
1024 Bytes	= 1 Kilobyte
1024 Kilobytes	= 1 Megabyte

Practise

1 State whether the following statements are true or false:
   a A byte is the smallest unit of storage in a computer.
   b One byte represents one character.
   c Each character has its own 8-bit binary code.
   d The binary code of an uppercase and a lowercase letter are the same.
   e Each computer uses its own code for each letter.

2 Work with a partner to put the following data storage units in order of size from the smallest to the largest:

(byte)   (megabyte)   (kilobyte)   (bit)

Keywords

kilobyte: a unit of digital storage or data equal to 1.024 bytes

megabyte: a unit of digital storage or data equal to 1.024 kilobytes

Types of storage

Learn

Every day we use different types of files: video, audio, graphics, pictures and text. All computers need to store this data on storage devices.

We need to know about different storage devices and how much they can store.

For example, computers used for video editing need a lot of storage because video files are very large.

Devices used for simple programs, or for writing letters, need much less storage space as these files are smaller.

Here are some common types of storage devices.

Hard Disk Drive (HDD)

These are one of the most common storage devices. They are normally found inside computer systems.

These devices can store a lot of data.

HDDs are used in computer systems because they are fast, available in very large capacities and are generally affordable.

Hard Disk Drive

Solid-State Drives (SSD)

These devices are inside a computer. They are a newer technology, replacing Hard Disk Drives.

SSDs are much faster than HDDs. This means they are better for playing the latest computer games or editing videos.

SSDs are quiet because they do not have any moving part

SSDs can store a lot of data. But they are more expensive than HDDs.

Solid State Drive

USB Flash Drives

USB Flash Drives are the most common type of portable storage.

They plug into any device with a USB port.

They are small and portable but have large storage capacities.

USB Flash Drive

Memory cards

This is another type of portable storage device that sits inside a device.

They are commonly used in electronic devices such as mobile phones, tablets, digital cameras, game consoles and MP3 players.

They are very small with a large storage capacity.

Memory Cards

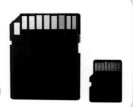

Discs

Optical discs were common in the past but are less common now.

They use light to store and find data on special discs. Different discs can store different amounts of data. For instance, a CD can hold 750 megabytes.

Optical discs are not used as much now because they cannot store as much data as other storage devices.

Optical Discs

Practise

1 State which of the following statements are true or false.

> **Keyword**
>
> **optical discs:** storage devices that use light to read and write data

   a   Optical storage devices are the most common storage device found in computer systems.

   b   SSDs cost more than HDDs.

   c   Memory cards are the main storage device in most computers.

   d   Digital cameras normally use HDDs to store photographs.

   e   HDDs are slower than SSDs.

2 Put each description in the correct column.

Description	HDD	SSD
More expensive		
Slower		
Noisier		
Usually stores more data		

3 Pia has a 2000-megabyte movie file stored on her computer that she wanted to transfer onto an optical storage device.

   a   Can Pia use a CD to store her movie? Explain your answer.

   b   What is the best storage device that Pia can transfer the movie file to, to be able to watch on other computers?

Go further

1 Work with your partner to complete the following:

   a Use the ASCII code table on page 38 to list the 8-bit binary code for the uppercase letter 'W' and the lowercase letter 'w'.

   b Discuss why you think the uppercase and lowercase for the same letter have different 8-bit binary codes.

   c Fill in the blank spaces below to describe what happens from the time the uppercase letter 'W' is pressed on the keyboard.

   If you are typing a report for your teacher on a computer, when the uppercase letter '____' on the keyboard is pressed it sends an electrical signal to the computer. The computer converts that electrical signal to the binary code _____. You see the uppercase letter '____' displayed on the screen but the computer sees the binary code _____.

2 Using the ASCII code table on page 38, write out your own name in binary code.

3 List three types of storage devices that can be used in a computer system.

4 Work with a partner to match the storage units to their respective storage file or device:

A	Byte
B	Kilobyte
C	Megabytes

1	Small text document
2	High quality photo
3	One character

Challenge yourself!

Copy the sentences and fill in the blanks using the words from the word bank below.

(characters) (secondary) (code) (kilobyte) (megabyte)

(number) (primary) (binary)

A computer is a device that represents data using the _____ number system. All _____ on a keyboard are associated with an 8-bit binary _____. A small text document requires about one _____, while a 1-minute audio in MP3 format requires about one _____ of storage space.

My project

Work in groups of 3–4.

Your parents do not understand how a computer stores data and how much storage space is required for different digital file types. They want to buy you a computer with a small HDD storage, but you want a more expensive computer with a larger SSD storage to play your games with 3D graphics.

1 Write a report to your parents to show and explain the following:
   a explain why computer systems use the binary number system to represent data
   b show a table comparing the different units used for computer storage
   c explain why a gaming computer requires more storage compared to other uses
   d state what SSD and HDD mean and justify why an SSD is better than an HDD for a gaming computer.

What can you do?

Read and review what you can do.
   ✔ I know that computers represent data in binary (1 or 0).
   ✔ I can identify bits, bytes, kilobytes and megabytes as units of memory size and storage.
   ✔ I can identify a range of storage devices that can be used within computer systems.

Creating stories

Get started!

In groups of 3 or 4, play the "Pass the story" game. In this game, one person starts a story and then the next person continues it, and so on.

An example is shown below.

Person 1 starts off the game.

Person 1 says: "Once upon a time …"

Person 2 continues the story by adding one sentence.

Person 2 says: "There was a little girl who loved bunnies."

Person 3 adds another sentence to continue the story.

Person 3 says: "She asked her parents if she could get a pet rabbit."

Person 1 (or 4) continues the story by adding another sentence.

Person 1 (or 4) says: "Her parents told her she can and they all went to the pet store."

And so on.

This continues until your teacher tells you to stop.

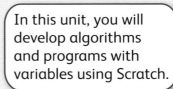

You will learn to:

- use variables in algorithms
- create a clear name for each variable
- develop programs with a variable
- write an outline plan for a program.

In this unit, you will develop algorithms and programs with variables using Scratch.

Warm up

Work in pairs. Look at the series of images for a story below.

A

B

C

D

E

F

Re-arrange the images in the correct sequence to tell a story that makes sense.

1 Image ___
2 Image ___
3 Image ___
4 Image ___
5 Image ___
6 Image ___

Compare your answer with your partner's.

Do you remember?

Before you start this unit, check that you:
- know how to develop algorithms where two objects interrelate
- know how to develop programs where two or more objects can interact.

In this unit, you will use Scratch.
There is an online chapter all about Scratch.

Algorithm to code
Understanding variables

Keywords

constant: a value that does not change

variable: a value that can change depending on certain conditions

Learn

There can be different types of data in algorithms and programs. For example, data can be numbers, text, dates and so on.

Data that does not change while a program or algorithm runs is called a constant. A constant may be typed into a program or assigned a name to identify it.

A variable is a value that can change when the program runs. Think of a variable as a container that holds different data at different times. For example, a variable may hold the value 7 at one point but later in the program, it holds the value 3.

Variables can be used to store numbers such as the score in a game, a count of something or the value of calculations. Variables can also store text such as people's names and addresses.

Look at the example below where one variable, called Name, is being used in an algorithm that displays a Hello message to the user.

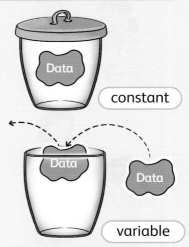

constant

variable

Example of an algorithm with a variable

Step	Instruction
1	Start
2	Create a variable called Name
3	Ask user to enter their name
4	Set variable, Name, to user's input in Step 3
5	Join 'Hello' + space + the variable name together
6	Output the result
7	End

In this algorithm, the user can enter any name. The variable stores whatever the user enters. The message that is displayed combines the word "Hello" with the data that the user enters.

For example, if the user enters "Jack", then the display message would be "Hello Jack". If the user enters "Jill", then the display message would be "Hello Jill". Each time the program is run, the value of the variable can change.

	User's input	Program's output
1st time program runs	Jack	Hello Jack
2nd time program runs	Jill	Hello Jill

Variables allow us to store and change data as an algorithm or program runs.

We must ensure that we create variables with clear names. It is important to use a clear and meaningful name for a variable so that:

- it correctly describes the variable's purpose
- it is easy for anyone else to understand what your program or algorithm is doing
- we can easily tell the difference between multiple variables.

Variable names should be unique and not too long. A variable's name should be exactly the same every time it is used in an algorithm or program. You need to take note of which letters in the name are uppercase, which are lowercase and if there are spaces.

Practise

1   Write an algorithm that displays a message to the user. The program should ask the user to enter their eye colour and then display the eye colour that was entered.

Step	Instruction
1	Start
2	Create a variable called _____
3	Ask user to enter _____
4	Set variable, _____, to user's input in Step _____
5	Join "You entered" and _____
6	_____
7	End

Hint: If the user enters "brown", then the message that is displayed is "You entered brown".

2   Create a variable in Scratch by following the steps below.

a   Choose a clear name for a variable to be assigned to text that a user enters as their name.

b   Open a new project and choose any sprite.

c   Click on the **Variables** group.

d   Click **Make a Variable** and type the name of your variable.

e   Click **OK** and check that the variable you created is listed.

The image shows a variable created called **Name**.

Variables can also store text, not just numbers!

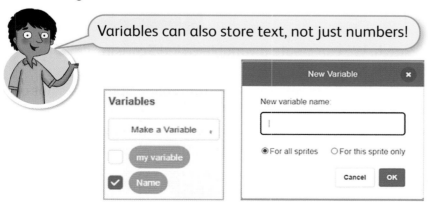

Variables in programs

We can create a variable called **Score** to store a player's points during a game. When the player scores a point, we can tell the program to increase the variable by one. As you collect more points, the value of this variable keeps changing.

Score = 0

Score = 1

Score = 2

Count = 2

We can also create a variable called **Count** to store the number of lives a player has. Every time a player dies, we can decrease the variable by one.

Count = 1

If the total number of lives is 2, then the variable can change from **2 to 1 to 0** and then the game ends.

Example of a variable in a program

Count = 0

Here is an algorithm for a **Duck** Sprite bouncing on a trampoline in a computer game. The algorithm includes a variable called **Score**, which stores the player's points. The first part of the algorithm sets the variable **Score** to 0. The second part of the algorithm increases the score by 1 every time the space key is pressed and the **Duck** jumps.

Computer programs can use variables to store information about a game.

Duck Sprite (Part 1)	
①	Start program when the Green Flag is clicked
②	Create a variable called Score
③	Set variable, Score, to 0

Duck Sprite (Part 2)	
①	Start program when the space key is pressed
②	Change y position by 40
③	Wait 0.2 seconds
④	Change y position by −40
⑤	Change variable, Score, by 1

We can create this algorithm in Scratch. We can create a variable called **Score** in Scratch. The code for the **Duck** Sprite is shown above.

The two sprites in this program are **Duck** and **Trampoline**. The **Trampoline** Sprite does not do anything. It is a static object and so it has no code.

We can see that if a player keeps pressing the space key, the score keeps increasing – from **0 to 1**, from **1 to 2**, from **2 to 3**, and so on.

Score = 0 → Score = 1 → Score = 2 → Score = 3

Practise

1 Create the program on the previous page as follows.

a Open a new project in Scratch.

b Add any backdrop.

c Search and select the **Trampoline** Sprite and position it in the middle of the stage.

d Select the **Duck** Sprite.

e Create a variable following the steps on page 48.

f Add the code on the previous page to the **Duck** Sprite.

g Test your program and check that you get the required results.

When you run your program, you should notice that the Score value on the screen increases every time you press the space key.

2 Create a program in Scratch with a variable assigned. It should do the following:

- The **Jordyn** Sprite should move one (1) step when the right arrow key is pressed and it should add one (1) to the count every time this happens.
- The program should start counting from 0.
- The **Basketball 2** Backdrop should be used.

a Choose a clear name for your variable and state what value is assigned to it.

b Write an algorithm for the sprite for:
  - when the Green Flag is clicked
  - when the right arrow key is pressed.

c Open a new project in Scratch.

d Add the correct backdrop.

e Add the correct sprite.

f Create the variable you chose in **a**.

g Create the code for your algorithm.

h Run the program and check the results.

Planning a program

Learn

We can write an outline plan for algorithms and programs by identifying:

- the purpose of the program
- the events that take place in a program
- the expected outcomes when the program runs.

We write a plan for each character in our program.

Keywords

event: a thing that happens or takes place

outcome: the result or way something turns out

subprogram: a small program that is part of the main program

Each **event** and its expected **outcome** can then be written as a **subprogram**.

Subprograms are small programs that are part of the larger, main program.

Subprograms perform a specific task that may or may not need to be repeated.

Example of writing an outline plan for a program

In this example, we have the task of creating a story in Scratch. In this program, there should be two sprites: **Dinosaur 3** and **Dinosaur 4**.

- The **Dinosaur 4** Sprite should say, "Hello!" for 2 seconds when the Green Flag is clicked
- The backdrop should switch to Jurassic when this **Dinosaur 4** is clicked on.

When the backdrop switches to Jurassic, the **Dinosaur 3** Sprite should:

- Glide for 1 second to a random position
- Say, "There's no place like home!" for 2 seconds.

When **Dinosaur 3** is clicked on:

- the backdrop should switch to Savanna
- **Dinosaur 3** should say "Let's explore!" for 2 seconds.

The first step in writing the outline plan is to identify the purpose of the program.

The purpose of this program is for two characters to react to certain inputs.

The second step is to identify the events.

There are four events that take place:

1   When the Green Flag is clicked
2   When the **Dinosaur 3** Sprite is clicked
3   When the **Dinosaur 4** Sprite is clicked
4   When the backdrop switches to Jurassic.

The final step is to identify the expected outcome for each event.

We can write this in algorithm form as shown below.

Dinosaur 4 Sprite (Part 1)	
①	Start program when the Green Flag is clicked
②	Say "Hello!" for 2 sec

Dinosaur 4 Sprite (Part 2)	
①	Start program when this sprite is clicked
②	Switch to Jurassic Backdrop

Dinosaur 3 Sprite (Part 1)	
①	Start program when backdrop switches to Jurassic
②	Glide 1s to a random position
③	Say "There's no place like home!" for 2 seconds

Dinosaur 3 Sprite (Part 2)	
①	Start program when this sprite is clicked
②	Switch to Savanna Backdrop
③	Say "Let's explore!" for 2 seconds

After planning the outline for our program, we can now write the subprograms for each part of the algorithm.

Practise

1 Create the program on the previous page as follows.

  a   Open a new project in Scratch.

  b   Add the Savanna Backdrop, then the Jurassic Backdrop.

  c   Search and select Dinosaur 4 and add the code below to this sprite.

  d   Search and select **Dinosaur 3** and add the code below to this sprite.

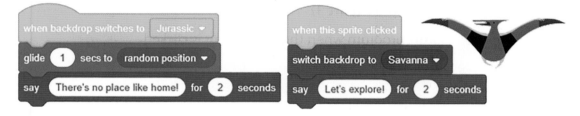

  e   Run your program and check that you get the required results.

2 Write an outline plan for a program for the following task:

  In this program, there should be two sprites, **Dinosaur 1** and **Dinosaur 2**.

  • The **Dinosaur 1** Sprite should say, "Hi" for 3 seconds when the Green Flag is clicked

  • The backdrop should switch to Jungle when **Dinosaur 1** is clicked on.

  • When the backdrop switches to Jungle, the **Dinosaur 2** Sprite should move 40 steps and then play a pop sound.

  When **Dinosaur 2** is clicked on,

  • the backdrop should switch to Forest

  • **Dinosaur 2** should say "Bye!" for 2 seconds.

Remember to include the purpose, events and expected outcomes (that is, an algorithm for each character).

Compare your answer with your partner.

Go further

1 Write an algorithm for the **Pico** Sprite in a program:

- **Pico** should jump when the space key is pressed by a change in y by 50, then wait 0.2 seconds and then have a change in y by −50.
- The program should count every time the **Pico** Sprite jumps.
- The variable should add one (1) to itself every time a jump happens.
- The program should start counting from 0 (the variable should start at 0).

Part 1	
①	Start program when …
②	
③	

Part 2	
①	Start program when …
②	
③	
④	
⑤	

2 Give two reasons why variables should have a clear name.
3 Create the program in Scratch for the algorithm in part **1**.
   - Search and select the **Pico** Sprite
   - Add the **Colorful City** Backdrop.
4 Test your code and check that you get the correct results.

Computational thinking

Write an algorithm with a variable that displays the user's name. It should:

- Ask the user for their name.
- Store that answer as a variable called **Name**.
- Display the word "Hello" and the value stored in the variable.

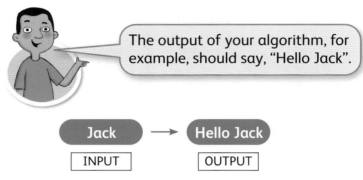

The output of your algorithm, for example, should say, "Hello Jack".

Jack → Hello Jack

INPUT   OUTPUT

5   Write an outline plan for a second character in your program as follows:

> The **Giga Walking** Sprite should say, "Hello!" when the Green Flag is clicked. The backdrop should switch to School when this sprite is clicked on. When the backdrop switches, **Giga Walking** should say, "Let's have fun at school!", then move 20 steps and then change its costume.

Remember to include the purpose, events and expected outcomes.

6   Create the program in Scratch for part **5**:
- Search and select the **Giga Walking** Sprite
- Add the **School** Backdrop.

7   Run your program and debug your code if needed.

Challenge yourself!

Make changes to your program from the **Go Further** activity.

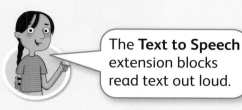

The **Text to Speech** extension blocks read text out loud.

Text to Speech
Make your projects talk.

Requires   Collaboration with
🛜   Amazon Web Services

1   Click the **Add Extension** button and add the **Text to Speech** Group to the Blocks Palette.

2   Add the code on the right to the Pico Sprite.

3   Add code to match the algorithm in the table to the **Giga Walking** Sprite.

Step	Instruction
❶	Start program when this sprite is clicked
❷	Switch to School Backdrop
❸	Set voice to squeak
❹	Speak "Yeah"

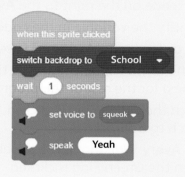

4   Add a third character to your program, the **Tera** Sprite.
    This sprite should give the results in the table.

Step	Instruction
❶	Start program when the Green Flag is clicked
❷	Switch to next costume
❸	Wait 3 seconds
❹	Hide

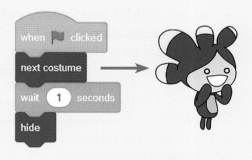

5   Debug the created code above to match the algorithm in the table and add the corrected code to the **Tera** Sprite.

6   Run your program and check that you get the required results.

My project

Create a story in Scratch where a character walks out of her bedroom to go to the refrigerator as follows.

1   Add these sprites and backdrops to a new project:
   - **Avery Walking** Sprite
   - **Milk** Sprite
   - **Cheesy Puffs** Sprite
   - **Bedroom 3** Backdrop
   - **Refrigerator** Backdrop

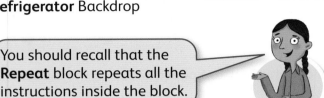

> You should recall that the **Repeat** block repeats all the instructions inside the block.

2   Add the code on the right to the **Avery Walking** Sprite.

3   a   Identify the variable in the code in part **2**.

   b   Is it a clear variable name? Give reasons for your answer.

4   Using the same variable name as the code in part **2**, write an outline plan (purpose, events, outcomes) for the rest of the program to get the following results:
   - When the Green Flag is clicked, the variable should be hidden and the backdrop should switch to **Bedroom 3**.
   - The **Avery Walking** Sprite should show on stage and go to position x = −175, y = −73 when the Green Flag is clicked.
   - The **Milk** and **Cheesy Puff** Sprites should hide when the Green Flag is clicked.
   - The **Milk** and **Cheesy Puff** Sprites should show when the backdrop switches to Refrigerator.
   - When the **Milk** and **Cheesy Puff** Sprites are clicked on, they should hide and the variable value should change by −1. (This means the variable should decrease by 1 every time this happens.)

Purpose:

Events:

> Run your program and check that you get the correct results; similar to the pictures shown on the next page.

Outcomes:

In the outcomes section, you should include algorithms for each event.

Part 1 (Backdrop)		Part 2 (Avery Walking Sprite)	

Part 3 (Milk Sprite)		Part 4 (Cheesy Puff Sprite)	

5 Create the program in Scratch for the algorithm in part **4**.

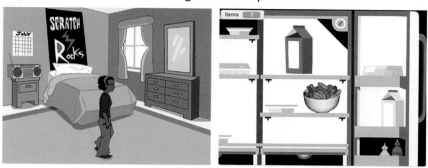

Did you know?

There are many different programming languages. Scratch is an example of a block-based programming language. There are also text-based programming languages; some of these are shown below.

Each programming language works differently with variables. Some require you to state the type of variable, such as whether it's a number or text.

What can you do?

Read and review what you can do.

✔ I can use variables in algorithms.

✔ I know that it is important to use a clear name for each variable.

✔ I can develop programs with a variable.

✔ I can identify the purpose, events and expected outcomes to write an outline plan for a program.

Great! Now, you can develop algorithms and programs with variables in Scratch.

Network devices

Get started!

Have you ever sent a letter to someone?

Sending things through the post lets users send documents and packages to an address in the same country or another country.

- Talk with your partner about how a letter reaches the intended address.
- What happens if the letter cannot be delivered to the intended address?

You will learn:

- the role of hardware in a network
- that all devices on a network have an IP address
- how websites are stored and accessed over the internet.

In this unit, you will learn about devices that make up a network, the role of an IP address and storing and accessing websites.

Warm up

Walk with your teacher around your school. Look at all the devices that are connected to the school's computer network.

Look at the cables and other devices in the computer room.

Draw the devices you have seen on a sheet of paper. Show how the cables are connected to the devices in your drawing.

Tell your partner the names of the different devices that you have seen in the computer room and other places in the school.

Do you remember?

Before you start this unit, check that you can:

- explain the role of servers and clients in a network
- describe the differences between the World Wide Web and the internet
- describe the differences between Wi-Fi® and ethernet.

Networks
Network devices

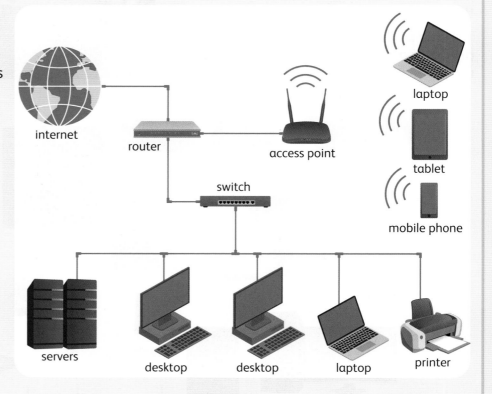

Learn

A computer network is a group of connected computers that can:

- 'talk' or communicate with one another
- share devices
- share data
- share software.

Networks need several types of hardware devices to work. Three of these devices are:

- switches
- Wi-Fi access points
- routers.

Switches

A network **switch** connects all the other devices in a network, allowing them to share information and communicate with one another.

The other devices connect to the switch using wires.

Devices that are connected to a switch include: computers, printers, scanners, gaming consoles, servers and Wi-Fi access points.

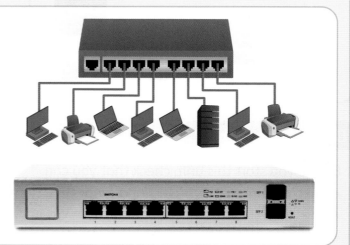

Access points

A **Wi-Fi access point** allows computers and other devices to connect to it wirelessly.

The access point is then connected to a network router or switch via a cable.

Access points are used to create a wireless network. Access points allows users to move from one location to another and continue to have wireless access to a network.

Access points can also increase the number of users that can connect to the same network.

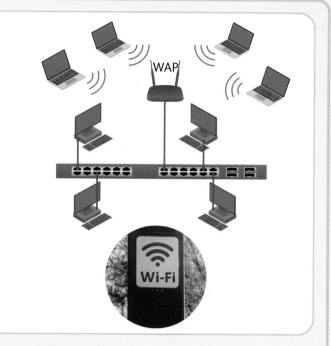

Routers

A **router** lets other devices connect to the internet. It allows several different devices to use the same internet connection.

A router sends data to and from the internet or between computers.

Routers can connect to more than one switch to form a larger network.

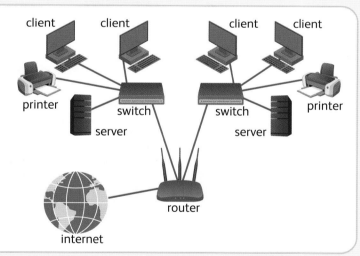

Keywords

switch: networking hardware that connects multiple devices on the same network and is able to receive and forward data to the specific destination device

Wi-Fi access point: a wireless network device that acts as a gateway for devices to connect to a network in a building, school or campus

router: a device that connects computers to the internet

For more about what a router does, see Unit 9.

Did you know?

Many modern routers have built-in switches and Wi-Fi access points.

Practise

1 State whether the following statements are true or false:

a A switch can connect to many devices in a network.

b A router can only be connected to one switch.

c A router allows the devices on the network to access the internet.

d All devices connected to an access point have to use wires.

e Access points can increase the number of users on a network.

f Switches allow connected devices to share information and communicate with one another.

2 Replace each label with one of the following words: **router**, **Wi-Fi access point** and **switch**.

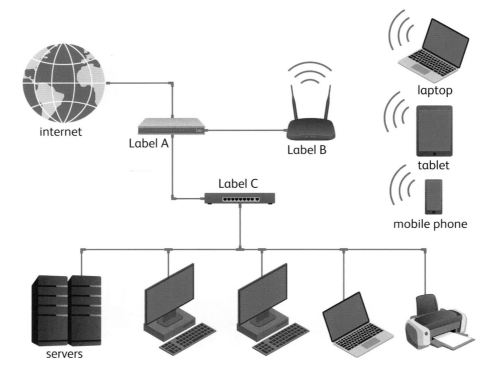

3 Write out these sentences and fill in the correct words in the blank spaces.

(switches) (router) (network) (switch) (Wi-Fi access point)

a A _____ connects all the network devices in a network.

b A _____ sends data to and from the internet. It can also be used to connect multiple _____ to form a large _____.

c A _____ can allow devices to connect to a network wirelessly.

IP Address

What is an IP address?

When you go online, for example to send emails, shop or chat, you send and receive data. This data must be sent to the correct destination and come back to your device.

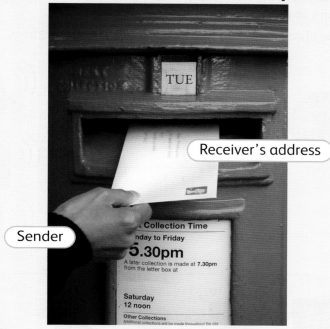

Receiver's address

Sender

To make this possible, each device connected to the internet is assigned a unique **IP address**. The IP address identifies the device on the network and on the internet.

An IP address has a similar role to your home address – it allows website, emails, and all other data to be delivered to your device.

An IP address consists of a string of four numbers separated by full stops. An example address is: **192.158.1.38**

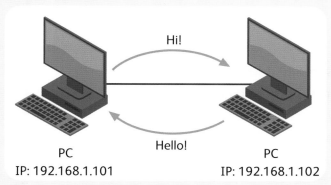

Hi!

Hello!

PC
IP: 192.168.1.101

PC
IP: 192.168.1.102

> **Keyword**
>
> **IP address:** a string of four numbers separated by full stops that identifies any device on a network. It allows devices to communicate with one another over the internet

All devices on the internet find, send and exchange information with other connected devices using their IP address.

Did you know?

How do IP addresses work?

Your device accesses the internet through a router, which is connected to the internet.

An IP address is assigned to your device by a router.

An IP address can change depending on where you are. For example, if you go to the library and you take your device with you, your home IP address does not come with you. This is because you are using another network to access the internet.

Instead, the router in the library network will assign a different IP address.

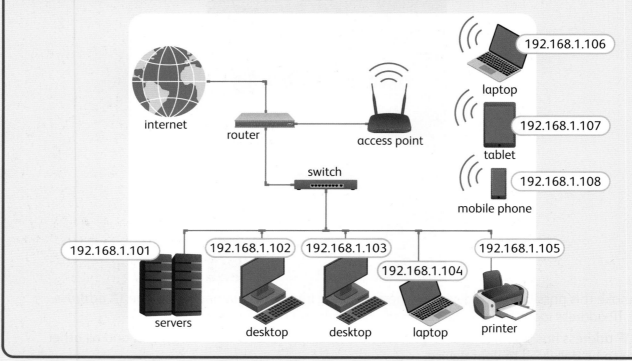

Practise

1 State whether the following statements are true or false:
   a   IP stands for Internet Protocol.
   b   Every computer on the internet has the same IP address.
   c   An IP address is a string of three numbers separated by full stops.
   d   Some devices on the internet do not have an IP address.
2 How many sets of numbers are contained in an IP address?
3 Tell your partner why each device has a unique IP address.

Storing and accessing websites

Learn

A web page is a way to display information from the internet. A collection of related web pages is called a website. For a website to be available to anyone, it needs to be stored on a computer or server that is connected to the internet.

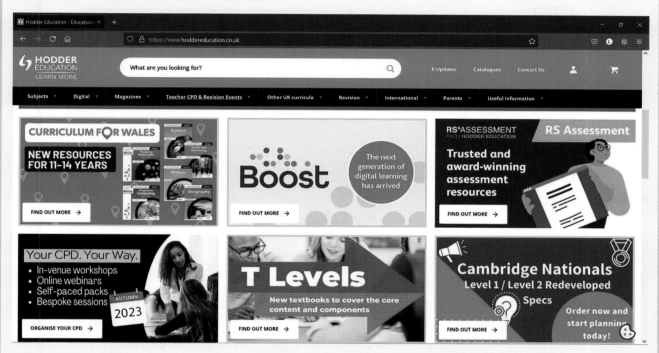

Each website has an address known as a **URL (uniform resource locator)**. The URL of a website is shown in the address bar of a browser (Mozilla, Chrome™, Microsoft Edge, and so on).

For example, the URL of Hodder Education is: https://www.hoddereducation.co.uk/

URL

The URL of Scratch is: https://scratch.mit.edu/

URLs are generally made up of letters, which makes it easy for people to remember them.

Computers, on the other hand, work with IP addresses. Computers need to turn a URL into an IP address.

Accessing a website

1 After a user types a URL, such as https://www.hoddereducation.co.uk/, into the browser and presses enter, the browser has to find the server on the internet that stores the website.

2 The browser sends the request to the router.

3 The router converts the URL into an IP address.

4 The request travels across the internet until it reaches a website server with the correct IP address.

5 The website server receives the request and sends a copy of the web page code to your browser to display.

6 Your web browser displays the page on your screen.

What is the URL for your school's website?

Did you know?

The first publicly available website was developed by Berners-Lee and became available on the internet on August 6, 1991. The site's URL was http://info.cern.ch.

Practise

1   State whether the following statements are true or false:
    a   A website can contain only one web page.
    b   Websites stored on computers not connected to the internet can be viewed by everyone.
    c   Each computer on the internet has a unique IP address.
    d   A website can be accessed by typing its URL into the address bar of a browser.
    e   A URL usually consists of letters.
    f   A URL must be converted to an IP address before it can be accessed.
2   Tell your partner the names of two popular browsers.
3   Give the URL of any website you have used.
4   Tell your partner how a website is viewed when you enter the URL into the address bar of your browser.

Go further

1   Which network device can connect all devices such as computers and printers?
2   Tell your partner two reasons why the principal of a school may want an access point to be installed on the network.
3   What does ISP stand for?
4   Explain to your friend the similarities between sending a letter using an addressed envelope and requesting information from a website from your computer.

Challenge yourself!

1   Tell your partner if you have internet at home, and if so, the names of the internet devices you have at your home.
2   a   If you have internet at home, find out which company provides this internet service.
    b   Find out which company provides internet services to your school.
3   Tell your partner how the devices at home are connected to the internet.

4   Jack wants to find out about the different types of horses. His friend sent him the following website: https://www.thesprucepets.com/

Tell your friend how a request for information from that website gets to your computer.

Can you find a way to find the IP address of this website?

My project

The principal of your school would like to build a computer network in the school. Provide your principal with the answers to the following questions:

What devices can be part of the school network?	
How would the devices be connected together?	
What device can be used to send data to designated computers?	
How would the network devices access the internet?	
Give one advantage of building a network.	
What would be one disadvantage of building a network?	
How can many people be given access to the network from anywhere on the school's grounds?	
Draw a sketch of the network. Include all of the devices that will be required and show how they will be connected together.	
Explain the steps involved if a computer on the network tried to access the website: www.unicef.org Make sure you explain any technical terms you use.	

What can you do?

Read and review what you can do.

✔ I can explain the role of switches, routers and Wi-Fi access points in a network.

✔ I know what an IP address is.

✔ I know why each device has a unique IP address.

✔ I can explain how websites are stored on servers and accessed over the internet.

Well done! Now you know the role of network devices on a network and how data is accessed from a server on the internet.

Making decisions

Get started!

Every day we make decisions based on different situations.

Tell your partner what decision you would make for each scenario below:

If my tablet battery is low, then I will _____.

If it is raining outside, then I will use an _____.

If the alarm clock rings, then it is time to _____.

If I am tired, then I will _____.

If the school bell rings, then it is time for _____.

If Cliff is thirsty, then he drinks water.

You will learn to:

- follow, understand and edit algorithms that contain selection
- predict the outcome of algorithms that contain selection
- plan the instructions for objects within a program.

In this unit, you will create programs with selection using Scratch.

Warm up

In groups of five, do the following:

1 Stand up in your group.

2 Take turns to read the instructions below, one at a time.

3 Listen carefully to each instruction and do as it says.

4 After each instruction, return to your normal standing position.

Instructions:

a If the month of your birthday ends with a 'Y' or 'R', then raise your right hand.

b If you can play a musical instrument, clap your hands three times.

c If you have black hair, touch your head.

d If your name ends with an 'A' or 'E', say 'Yes!'

e If your eyes are brown, point to your eyes.

f If you can ride a bicycle, then jump two times.

g If you have a pet, make an animal sound.

h If you have a brother or sister, touch your toes.

i If your favourite ice-cream flavour is vanilla, give a thumbs up.

j If you can play cricket, then strike a pose.

Meow!

Do you remember?

Before you start this unit, check that you can:

- predict the outcome of algorithms with repetition
- develop programs with repetition
- develop programs that reset objects to their original state
- create programs with multiple algorithms running at the same time.

There is an online chapter all about **Scratch**.

Algorithms with selection

Algorithms are a set of step-by-step instructions to complete a task or solve a problem.

Sometimes in an algorithm, you may reach a step where a decision needs to be made. The result of the decision can lead to different outcomes.

Decisions are known as **selection**. Selection allows us to ask a question to determine which path to take next.

Two types of selection statements are:

- If ... Then
- If ... Then ... Else

These statements are also called **conditional** statements. In this unit, we will be looking at **If ... Then** statements. There are two parts to this statement:

1   Condition (after 'If')

2   Conclusion (after 'Then').

The conclusion statement is only carried out if the condition is **true**.

Every day we make **If ...Then** decisions based on conditions. For example,

'**If** the weather is sunny, **Then** I will go outside to play cricket.'

Condition   Conclusion

Algorithms with the If ... Then statement

Algorithm 1	
Step	**Instruction**
①	Start program when sprite is clicked
②	Go to a random position
③	**3.1** If sprite is touching the edge of the screen, then
	3.1.1 Switch to the next costume
④	Stop program

Let's look at Algorithm 1.

Step 2 The sprite will move to a random position every time the mouse clicks on it.

Step 3.1 The **condition** is: sprite touching the edge of the screen.

Step 3.1.1 The **conclusion** is: the sprite will switch to its next costume.

Note that step 2 is always carried out.

Step 3.1.1 Is only carried out if the sprite is touching the edge of the screen.

> **Keywords**
>
> **selection:** a decision taken based on information
>
> **conditional:** subject to a condition being met

Algorithm 2	
Step	**Instruction**
①	Start program when sprite is clicked
②	Go to a random position
③	**3.1** If sprite is touching the edge of the screen, then
	3.1.1 Switch to the next costume
	3.1.2 Say 'Hello' for 2 seconds
	3.1.3 Turn 45˚ to the right
④	Stop program

We can add additional conclusions within the **If … Then** statement, as seen in Algorithm 2.

Step 3.1.1 Conclusion 1: The sprite will switch to its next costume.

Step 3.1.2 Conclusion 2: The sprite will say 'Hello' for 2 seconds

Step 3.1.3 Conclusion 3: The sprite will turn 45 degrees to the right

If the condition in Step 3.1 is true, all three conclusions within the **If … Then** statement will be performed. If the condition is **not** true, the conclusions will not be performed and the program will end.

Practise

1 Look at the following **If … Then** statements. Identify the condition and the conclusion.

  a If I am hungry, then I will eat.

  b If a polygon has 3 sides, then it is a triangle.

  c If I complete my homework, then I can play video games.

  d If it is raining, then I will stay indoors.

  e If it is my birthday, then I will get cake.

2 a Complete the algorithms below to show that when the Green Flag is clicked, the **Butterfly** glides for 1 second towards the **Bat**. If the **Bat** touches the **Butterfly**, then the **Bat** will go to a random position.

Algorithm for the Butterfly	
Step	**Instruction**
①	Start when _____
②	Glide for _____ second to _____
③	Stop program

Algorithm for the Bat	
Step	**Instruction**
①	Start when _____
②	Wait 1 second
③	**3.1** If the _____ is touching the _____, then
	3.1.1 Go to a _____
④	Stop program

  b Identify the condition and the conclusion in the **Algorithm for the Bat**.

  c Edit the **Algorithm for the Butterfly** to repeat Step 2 five times in total.

  d Edit the **Algorithm for the Bat** to repeat Steps 2 and 3 five times in total.

Predict outcomes with selection

Algorithms that contain an **If… Then** statement have two possible outcomes:

Outcome 1: When the condition is true

Outcome 2: When the condition is not true

For example, look at the algorithm below for a moving **Balloon**. We can predict the outcomes of this algorithm:

Algorithm for a moving Balloon	
Step	**Instruction**
①	Start program when space key is pressed
②	Show Balloon on screen
③	Set Balloon to glide 2 seconds to random position
④	**4.1** If Balloon is touching Hedgehog, then
	4.1.1 Hide Balloon on screen
	4.1.2 Play the 'Pop' sound until done
⑤	Repeat steps 3 and 4 forever
⑥	Stop program

When the space key is pressed:

The **Balloon** glides for 2 seconds to a random position on the screen.

Outcome 1 – Condition is true

If the **Balloon** is touching the **Hedgehog** then the **Balloon** disappears (4.1.1) and the 'Pop' sound will play (4.1.2). The program will only end when the Stop button is clicked.

Outcome 2 – Condition is not true

If the **Balloon** is not touching the **Hedgehog**, then steps 4.1.1 and 4.1.2 are not carried out and the program goes straight to Step 5.

The result is that the Balloon will repeatedly glide around the screen to random positions until it touches the Hedgehog, when it disappears. The program will only end when the Stop button is clicked.

> The **Hedgehog** is a static object in the program.

> The **repeat forever** instruction in Step 5 means the program will indefinitely check to see when the **Balloon** touches the **Hedgehog**. If it does, the **Balloon** disappears. It only reappears when the program is stopped and run again.

Keywords

predict: to say what will happen in the future

indefinite: lasting for an unknown length of time

Practise

1 Identify the condition and conclusions for each algorithm below.

2 Predict the outcomes of each algorithm.

Algorithm for a Balloon	
Step	**Instruction**
1	Start program when up arrow key is pressed
2	Show Balloon on screen
3	Set Balloon size to 20%
4	Increase Balloon size by 20
5	Wait 1 second
6	**6.1** If Balloon is touching Mouse pointer, then
	6.1.1 Hide Balloon on screen
	6.1.2 Play the 'Pop' sound until done
7	Repeat steps 4 to 6 forever
8	Stop program

Algorithm for Avery	
Step	**Instruction**
1	Start program when Green Flag is clicked
2	Set Avery position to x = –170, y = –13
3	Move 20 steps forward
4	Change to the next Avery walking costume
5	Wait 0.5 seconds
6	**6.1** If Avery is touching Abby, then
	6.1.1 Say 'Hello'
7	Repeat steps 3 to 6 forever
8	Stop program

> Abby is a static object in the program.

Program planning

Keyword

static object: does not have any code

Learn

Creating programs with an If ... Then statement

Programs with selection are more complicated. We need to create a plan for each object within the program before we create the code.

The steps below show how to plan the instructions for an object in a program:

1 Identify the purpose of the object. Ask yourself the following questions:

   a Is it a **static object**? If yes, then the object does not move from its starting position.

   b Does the object need to perform any actions? If yes, then list what these actions are.

2 Identify the inputs for the object. For example: **Start program when this sprite is clicked**.

3 Identify the **conditions** that need to be met.

4 Identify the **conclusions** of the condition.

5 Write the algorithm for the object.

6 Using the algorithm, create the code for the object.

7 Test and debug your code.

Using the **Algorithm for a moving Balloon** on page 74, we can identify the following:

For the **Balloon1** sprite:

1 Is it a static object? No

2 Is the object required to perform any actions? The Balloon is required to glide for 2 seconds to a random position on the screen. This is repeated forever.

3 Input: when the space key is pressed

4 Condition that needs to be met: **Balloon** is touching the Hedgehog

5 Conclusions of the condition:

   Conclusion 1: **Balloon** is hidden

   Conclusion 2: a Pop sound is played

For the **Hedgehog** sprite:

6 Is it a static object? Yes

7 Is the object required to perform any actions? No

Creating the code for the Balloon1 sprite

The steps below show how to create the code for the **Balloon**:

1   Create a new project on Scratch and delete Sprite 1.

2   Search and select the **Blue Sky** backdrop.

3   Search and select the **Balloon1** and **Hedgehog** sprites.

4   Under the Events group of blocks, select the **when () key pressed** block. Click on the dropdown arrow and select **space**.

5   Under the **Looks** group of blocks, add the show block to the programming area.

6   Under the **Control** group of blocks, add the forever block to the show block.

7   Under the **Motion** group of blocks, select the glide () secs to () block. Change the number from 1 to **2**. Click on the dropdown arrow and select random position. Add this block inside the **forever** block.

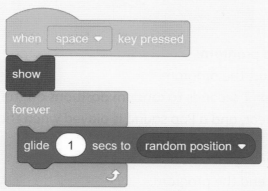

8   Under the **Control** group of blocks, select the **if () then** block. Add this block after the **glide () secs to ()** block, inside the **forever** block.

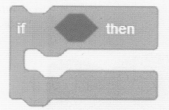

9   Add the **touching ()** block from the **Sensing** group to the hexagon area in the **if () then** block. Click on the dropdown arrow and select **Hedgehog**.

10 Add the **hide** block from the **Looks** group inside the **if () then** block.

11 Under the **Sound** group of blocks, add the **play sound () until done** block to the **hide** block. The Pop sound is selected by default. The final code is shown:

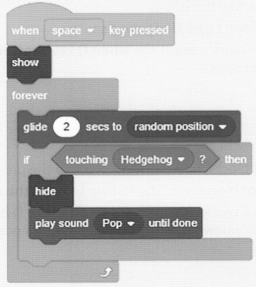

Testing and debugging the program:

1   Press the space key to start the program.

2   Does the Balloon glide for 2 seconds to random positions on the screen?

3   Does the Balloon disappear, and a Pop sound is played when the **Balloon** touches the **Hedgehog**?

    If not, check the code for any errors and correct it.

4   Click the Stop button to end the program.

> If the balloon touches the hedgehog it should disappear and you should hear a 'pop' sound.

Practise

1   Using the algorithm for the **Balloon** on page 75, answer the following questions:
   a   Is the **Balloon** a static object?
   b   What is the input in the **Balloon** algorithm?
   c   What is the condition that needs to be met?
   d   What are the conclusions?

2   Create the code for the **Balloon**:
   a   Create a new project in Scratch and delete **Sprite 1**.
   b   Search and select the **Blue Sky 2** Backdrop.
   c   Search and select the **Balloon 1** Sprite.
   d   Add the **when () key pressed** block. Select **up arrow**.
   e   Add the **show** block.
   f   Add the **set size** to block. Change the number to 20 %.
   g   Add the **forever** block.
   h   Add **change size by** block inside the **forever** block. Change the number to 20.
   i   Add the **wait** block inside the **forever** block.
   j   Add the **if () then** block inside the **forever** block.
   k   Under the **Sensing** group of blocks, add the **touching (mouse pointer)** block to the hexagon area in the **if () then** block.

   l   Add the **hide** block inside the **if () then** block.
   m   Add **play sound () until done** block inside the **if () then** block. Select the **pop** sound.

The **set size** to and **change size by** blocks are found in the **Looks** group.

3   Run your code by pressing the **up arrow**. Leave the mouse pointer somewhere near the **Balloon**. What do you observe?

4   Did your **Balloon** disappear, and a **pop** sound was heard? If not, check your code for any errors. Correct them.

Go further

Computational thinking

1 Look at the algorithms for the **Diver** and **Jellyfish**. Predict the outcomes of the **Algorithm for the Diver**.

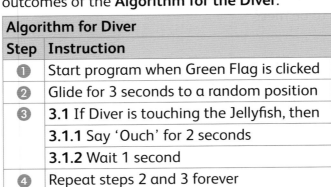

Algorithm for Diver	
Step	**Instruction**
①	Start program when Green Flag is clicked
②	Glide for 3 seconds to a random position
③	**3.1** If Diver is touching the Jellyfish, then
	3.1.1 Say 'Ouch' for 2 seconds
	3.1.2 Wait 1 second
④	Repeat steps 2 and 3 forever
⑤	Stop program

Algorithm for Jellyfish	
Step	**Instruction**
①	Start program when Green Flag is clicked
②	Go to x = −16, y = 58
③	Stop program

2 Using the algorithms for the **Diver** and the **Jellyfish**, answer the following questions:

a Is the **Diver** a static object?

b Is the **Jellyfish** a static object?

c What is the input for each sprite?

d What are the condition and conclusions for the **Diver** Sprite?

3 Create the program for the **Diver** and **Jellyfish**:

a Create a new project on Scratch and delete **Sprite 1**.

b Search and select the **Underwater 1** Backdrop.

c Search and select the **Diver 1** Sprite.

d Add the blocks of code for the **Diver 1** Sprite.

e Search and select the **Jellyfish** Sprite.

f Add the blocks of code for the **Jellyfish** Sprite.

g Test and debug the program.

h Was your prediction in question **1** correct?

The **say () for () seconds** block is found in the **Looks** group. Change the word 'Hello!' to 'Ouch'.

say Hello! for 2 seconds

Challenge yourself!

Computational thinking

1 Look at Algorithms 1 and 3. Predict the outcome of each algorithm when the Green Flag is clicked.

2 Predict the outcome of Algorithm 2 for the **Food Truck**.

3 Predict the outcome of Algorithm 4 for **Devin**.

Algorithms for the Food Truck

Algorithm 1	
Step	**Instruction**
❶	Start program when Green Flag is clicked
❷	Set size to 50 %
❸	Go to x = –176, y = –115
❹	Stop program

Algorithm 2	
Step	**Instruction**
❶	Start program when any key is pressed
❷	**2.1** If the space key is pressed, then
	2.1.1 Glide 5 seconds to x = 193, y = –115
	2.1.2 Play sound car horn until done
❸	Stop program

Algorithms for Devin

Algorithm 3	
Step	**Instruction**
❶	Start program when Green Flag is clicked
❷	Set size to 50 %
❸	Go to x = 193, y = –73
❹	Stop program

Algorithm 4	
Step	**Instruction**
❶	Start program when 's' key is pressed
❷	**2.1 If** Devin is touching Food Truck, then
	2.1.1 Say 'Stop!' For 2 seconds
❸	Stop program

4   Using the algorithms for the **Food Truck** and **Devin**, answer the following questions:

   a   Is the **Food Truck** a static object?

   b   Is **Devin** a static object?

   c   What is the input to set the sprites to their starting position?

   d   What are the input, condition and conclusions for Algorithm 2?

   e   What is the input, condition and conclusion for Algorithm 4?

5   Create the program for the **Food Truck** and **Devin**:

   a   Create a new project in Scratch and delete **Sprite 1**.

   b   Search and select the **Colorful City** Backdrop.

   c   Search and select the **Food Truck** Sprite.

   d   Add the blocks of code for Algorithms 1 and 2 to the **Food Truck** Sprite.

   e   Search and select the **Devin** Sprite.

   f   Add the blocks of code for Algorithms 3 and 4 to the **Devin** Sprite.

   g   Click the Green Flag to start the program.

   h   Press the space key. What happens?

   i   Press the 's' key to run the code for **Devin**.

   j   Were your predictions in questions **2** and **3** correct?

Algorithms 1 and 3 reset the **Food Truck** and **Devin** back to their original state when the Green Flag is clicked.

My project

Computational thinking

Look at Algorithms 6 and 8 for the **Crab** and **Toucan**.

1 Predict the outcome for the **Crab**.

2 Predict the outcome for the **Toucan**.

Algorithms for Crab

Algorithm 5	
Step	**Instruction**
❶	Start program when Green Flag is clicked
❷	Go to x = −161, y = −153
❸	Switch costume to Crab-a
❹	Stop program

Algorithm 6	
Step	**Instruction**
❶	Start program when 'm' key is pressed
❷	Glide 3 seconds to x = 93, y = 7
❸	Switch costume to Crab-b
❹	Stop program

Algorithms for Toucan

Algorithm 7	
Step	**Instruction**
❶	Start program when Green Flag is clicked
❷	Go to x = 93, y = 7
❸	Switch costume to Toucan-a
❹	Stop program

Algorithm 8	
Step	**Instruction**
❶	Start program when 'm' key is pressed
❷	**2.1 If** Toucan is touching the Crab, then
	2.1.1 Next costume
	2.1.2 Glide 1 second to x = 167, y = 138
	2.1.3 Next costume
❸	Repeat step 2 forever
❹	Stop program

3 Using the algorithms for the **Crab**:

    a What are the inputs for Algorithms 5 and 6?

    b Is the **Crab** a static object?

4 Write a plan for the **Toucan** using Algorithms 7 and 8.

5 Create the program for the **Crab** and the **Toucan**:

    a Create a new project in Scratch and delete **Sprite 1**.

    b Search and select the **Beach Malibu** Backdrop.

    c Search and select the **Crab** Sprite.

    d Add the blocks of code for Algorithms 5 and 6 to the **Crab** Sprite.

    e Search and select the **Toucan** Sprite.

    f Add the blocks of code for Algorithms 7 and 8 to the **Toucan** Sprite.

    g Click the Green Flag to start the program.

    h Press the 'm' key. What do you observe?

    i Were your predictions in questions **1** and **2** correct?

Did you know?

In programming, the **If ... Then** statement is commonly used in creating a password for an application or system. If the user enters the correct password, then they can access the application or system. What would happen if you entered the wrong password for your Scratch user account?

Join Scratch

Create projects, share ideas, make friends. It's free!

Create a username

Xaviera2022

Create a password

Scratch@3

Scratch@3

☑ Show password

Next

What can you do?

Read and review what you can do.

✔ I can follow, understand and edit algorithms that contain selection.

✔ I can predict the outcome of algorithms with selection.

✔ I can plan the instructions for objects within a program.

Well done! Now you can create programs with selection in Scratch!

Mathematical operators

Get started!

Work with your partner to answer the following questions.

Table 1 has data. Table 2 shows the **mathematical operators** and their symbols.

Table 1

Items	Amount sold
Red ink pens	12
Blue ink pens	5
Black ink pens	7

Keyword

mathematical operators: examples include adding, subtracting, multiplying and dividing

Table 2

Mathematical operators	Symbol
Add	+
Subtract	−
Multiply	×
Divide	÷

1   Which mathematical operator will be used to find the total amount of items sold?

2   Find the sum of the pens sold. Refer to Table 1 for the numbers.

3   Which mathematical operator will be used to find the difference between the number of red ink pens and blue ink pens sold?

4   Find the difference between the number of red ink pens and black ink pens sold. Refer to Table 1 for the numbers.

You will learn:

• to make cells only accept specific data types

• about formulae and functions in spreadsheets

• that cell references are used when data might change

• how to find data.

In this unit, you will learn about data types, formulae and how to find data.

Warm up

Work with your partner. Here is a table with some data.

Fruit	Unit cost	Quantity sold	Total cost of fruits sold
Apples	$0.50	5	$ 2.50
Pears	$2.00	8	$16.00
Oranges	$1.00	12	$12.00
		Grand Total	$30.50

1   Copy the table above in your notebook.

2   Change the quantity of pears bought from 8 to 10.

3   Recalculate the **Grand Total** cost of the fruits sold.

4   a   Which numbers were affected by the change in the quantity of pears sold?

    b   Explain how these numbers were affected.

If you had used a spreadsheet, then the Grand Total could be recalculated automatically. This is one of the benefits of using a spreadsheet.

Do you remember?

Before you start this unit, check that you:

- know about the structure of a spreadsheet
- know how to identify appropriate data types for a field
- can identify data, records and fields within a data table
- know how to use a database table to answer a question.

Performing calculations
Mathematical operators

One advantage of using a spreadsheet is that you can easily perform calculations. Calculations are carried out using a **formula**.

All formulae start with an equal sign and can include:

- Cell references – the data in the cell is used in the calculation.
- Mathematical symbols (+, −, *, /) – used to perform an operation.
- Constants – a value that does not change. For example, the formula for the perimeter of a rectangle is:

(Length + Width) × 2

The number 2 in the formula is an example of a constant.

The table shows the mathematical operators and symbols.

Look at the formula in the spreadsheet to add the numbers 4 and 2.

Formulae is the plural of formula!

Mathematical operator	Symbol
Add	+
Subtract	−
Divide	/
Multiply	*

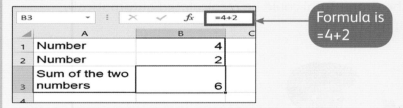

Formula is =4+2

The formula **=4+2** is entered in cell B3.

After pressing Enter, the sum **6** is seen in cell B3. The formula **=4+2** is seen in the formula bar.

Write the formula to be used in a spreadsheet to:

- calculate the difference between 4 and 2. Use the operator =
- multiply 4 and 2. Use the operator *
- divide 4 by 2. Use the operator /

What happens if we change the value 4 to 5 in the spreadsheet?

The sum would be wrong because the formula remains the same (=4+2).

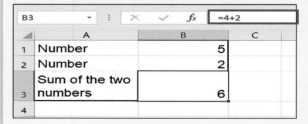

Keyword

cell reference: also known as cell address, is identified by a column letter and row number

We can use **cell references** instead of actual values in formulae. If a value in a cell is changed, the formula automatically uses the updated value to calculate a new result.

Look at the same calculation, but this time using cell references.

The value 4 is in cell B1. The value 2 is in cell B2. In cell B3, we will type **=B1+B2**, then press the Enter key.

The sum is **6**, as before. The formula **=B1+B2** is seen in the formula bar.

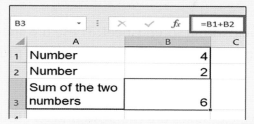

Let's change 4 to 5 in cell B1. Cell B3 automatically changes to the correct answer, 7.

The formula used the new value, 5, in cell B1.

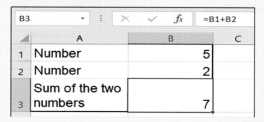

Practise

Work in small groups.

1 Enter the data in a spreadsheet as seen.

2 Perform the following calculations. The first one is done for you.

    a In cell C1, enter the formula to find the sum of the two numbers, 20 and 5.

       For example **=A1+B1**

	A	B	C
1	20	5	= A1+B1
2	20	5	
3	20	5	
4	20	5	

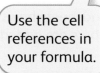

Use the cell references in your formula.

    b In cell C2, enter the formula to find the difference between the two numbers, 20 and 5.

    c In cell C3, enter the formula to multiply 20 by 5.

    d In cell C4, enter the formula to divide 20 by 5.

3 Change the value in cell B1 to **15**. In your notebook, state what happens when the value is changed from 5 to 15.

Performing calculations
Functions

Learn

Some formulae are already built into a spreadsheet. These are known as **functions**.

Functions consist of an equals sign, the function name and the **argument** (which is a range of cells enclosed in brackets).

A function is easier to use when there are a lot of values.

There are many functions, two examples are the **SUM** and **AVERAGE** functions.

SUM function

The SUM function adds all the values in a range of cells.

In the previous example, the numbers 5 and 2 were added to get the sum 7, using the operator +.

The same calculation can be performed using the SUM function. The formula will be:

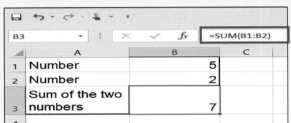

Equal sign

Function

Argument

Notice that the maths symbols are not needed when using a function.

AVERAGE function

The AVERAGE function finds the **mean** of all the values in the argument.

This spreadsheet shows the **formula** to find the mean of the three numbers, 10, 3 and 2. The numbers are added and then divided by 3.

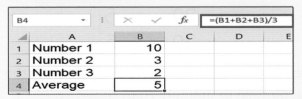

This spreadsheet shows the AVERAGE function to calculate the mean of the same three numbers.

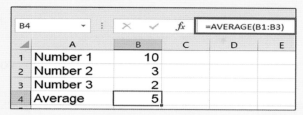

| B4 | | ⋮ | ✕ | ✓ | *fx* | =AVERAGE(B1:B3) |

	A	B	C	D	E
1	Number 1	10			
2	Number 2	3			
3	Number 3	2			
4	Average	5			

Keywords

argument: the cells containing data to be used in a function

mean: the average value amongst a set of values. It is found by adding all values and then dividing by the number of values that are added

Practise

1 Copy the numbers below into a spreadsheet. Enter the labels SUM in cell A7 and AVERAGE in cell A8.

a Enter the formula in cell B7 to calculate the sum of all the numbers. Use the SUM function.

Complete the formula =___(B1:_)

b Enter the formula in cell B8 to calculate the average of the numbers. Use the AVERAGE function.

Complete the formula =___(_:B_)

	A	B	C
1		6	
2		9	
3		8	
4		25	
5		13	
6		40	
7	SUM		
8	AVERAGE		
9			

Cells
Data validation

The cells in a spreadsheet can be set to ensure that the data entered is **valid**. For example, setting the data type controls what type of data can be entered in a cell.

Several data types are allowed in spreadsheets. Three of these data types are:

- **Numbers** – values, for example: 1, 25.5, 18
- **Text** – a set of characters such as letters, numbers and symbols, for example Jill Sanders, ST001, 3F!
- **Dates** – only dates are allowed, for example 06/18/2022.

The spreadsheet below shows how to set a data type using the **Data Validation** feature.

- First, the range of cells with the data is selected.
- The **Data Tab – Data Validation Group** is then selected.
- The **Settings** tab shows the data types that are allowed.

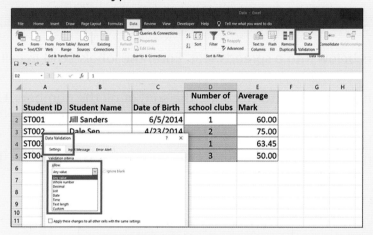

Once the data type is selected, the **Data** menu lets us set data that meet a condition, such as less than, between, equal to, and so on.

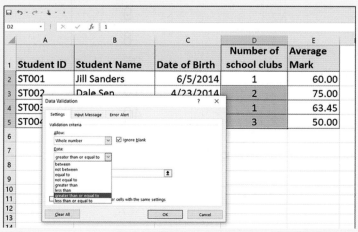

The examples below show what happens if data that is not **valid** is entered in a cell.

Numbers: Any data input that is not a number will not be allowed.

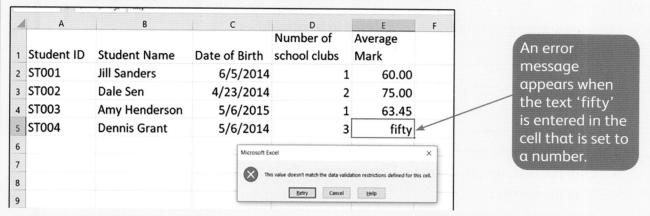

An error message appears when the text 'fifty' is entered in the cell that is set to a number.

Dates: If you attempt to enter data that is not of the **Date** data type, you will not be allowed to move to the next cell until the correct data type is entered.

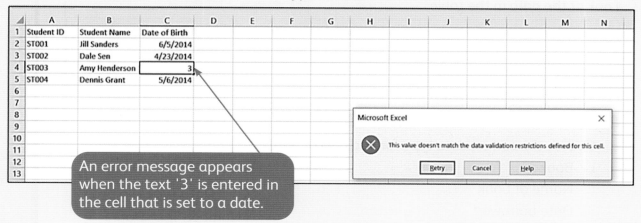

An error message appears when the text '3' is entered in the cell that is set to a date.

Text: Only text is allowed in these cells. You can also set a limit to the length of text. This is useful when entering codes or IDs of a certain length, such as zip or postal codes.

In this example, the Student ID cells A2 to A5 are restricted to a length of six characters.
A message indicating 'Incorrect Student ID' appears if a length of six characters is not entered.

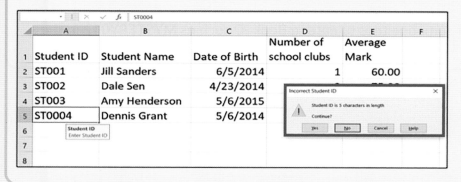

Keyword
valid: acceptable

Practise

Work in pairs.

1 Here are some data that must be entered in a spreadsheet.

Club ID	Club name	Number of members
ROB01	Robotics	35
MAT01	2	Fifteen
SWI02	Swimming	40

The following fields were set given the criteria below:

- Club ID: **text**, length of text – 5 characters
- Club name: **text**
- Number of members: **number**

Which data in the table above will lead to an error during data entry?

2 Look at the data in the table.

Book ID	Name of book	Date borrowed	Number of books remaining
FICT001	Matilda	6/12/2023	10
SCIE005	Science You can Eat	6/3/2023	5
THRI020	Spy School	6/10/2023	2

a Choose the correct data type for each set of data:
  i Book ID
  ii Name of book
  iii Date borrowed
  iv Number of books remaining

> **Data types**
>
> Number, Text, Date

b What is the length of the Book ID field?
  i 3
  ii 4
  iii 7

c What would happen if someone tries to enter a Book ID such as **MYSTERY012** in the Book ID field?

Searching for data
Using a filter

Learn

Filtering data in a spreadsheet lets you find data you want. When you filter data, entire rows will be hidden if the values do not match the filter criteria.

Here are some of the ways to filter records in a spreadsheet.

Filtering data that matches a criterion

The data table shows the details of items at a supermarket.

We will filter the table to find all items that are less than $5.00.

Criterion: Item price less than $5.00

STEPS

1. Go to any cell in the data table.
2. Click on the **Data** Tab.
3. Click on the **Filter** icon.
4. Click the drop-down arrow in the **Item price** column.
5. Click on the **Number Filters** option.
6. Click on **Less Than** in the drop-down menu.

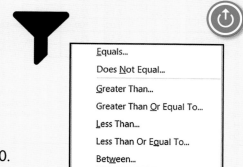

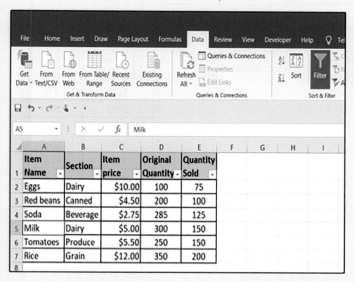

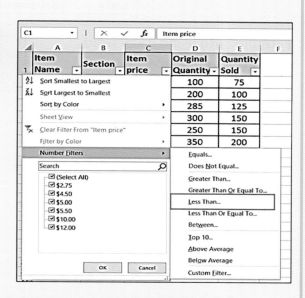

Keywords

filtering: only showing data that matches particular criteria

criteria: the conditions for a decision (Note: **criterion** is the singular of criteria.)

7   Click on the drop-down arrow to select the item price $5.00.

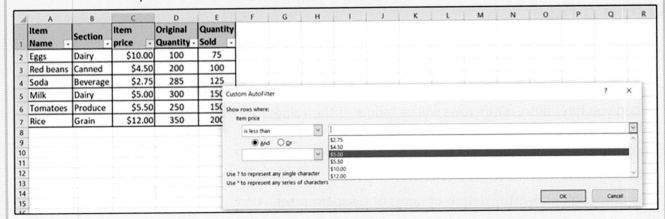

8   Click OK.

The data table will be filtered to show only the records with item prices less than $5.00.

There are only two items that are less than $5.00.

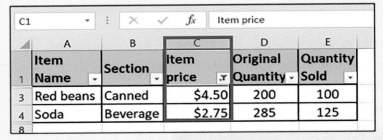

Filtering data using a key word

We can also filter for specific words.

Criterion: <u>All 'dairy' items</u>

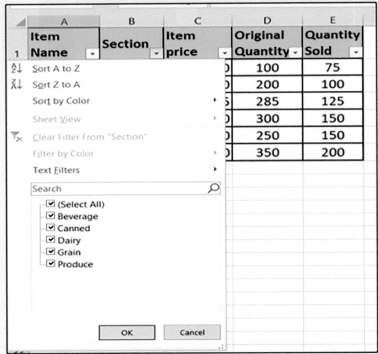

STEPS

1   Go to any cell in the data table.
2   Click on the **Data** Tab
3   Click on the **Filter** icon.
4   Click the drop-down arrow in the **Section** field.
5   Type the key word **Dairy** in the **Search** box.
6   Click OK.

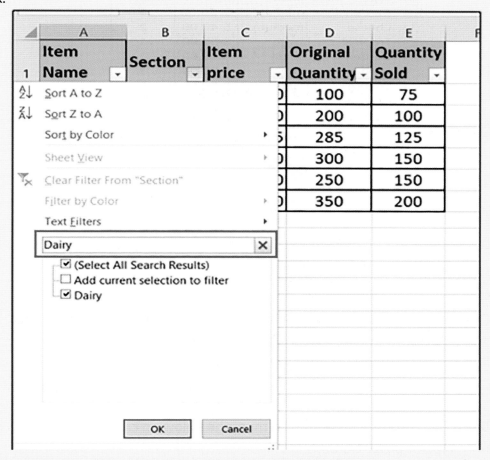

7   The data table will be filtered to show only the records with 'dairy' items.

	A Item Name	B Section	C Item price	D Original Quantity	E Quantity Sold
2	Eggs	Dairy	$10.00	100	75
5	Milk	Dairy	$5.00	300	150
8					

Practise

1   Work in pairs for this activity. Copy the data shown below into a spreadsheet.

	A	B	C	D	E
1	Type of pizza	Size of pizza	Cost of pizza	Number ordered	
2	Garden	medium	$ 35.00	1	
3	Cheese	medium	$ 40.00	2	
4	Tropical	large	$ 55.00	1	
5	Garden	small	$ 25.00	2	
6	Garden	large	$ 50.00	3	
7	Cheese	large	$ 50.00	7	
8	Cheese	medium	$ 40.00	4	
9					

Use a filter to find records with data that meet the following criteria.

a   Criterion: Type of pizza: Garden

b   Criterion: Pizzas that cost less than $40.00

c   Criterion: All medium-sized pizzas

d   Criterion: Number of pizzas ordered – more than 3

Refer to the **Learn** panel if you need help with the steps.

Go further

Work in small groups. Use this spreadsheet on Students' Test Scores to answer the questions below.

Students' Test Scores

	A	B	C	D	E	F
	E6		f_x			
1	Name of Student	Date Test Taken	Math Mark	Science Mark	Total	
2	Judy Andrews	6/21/2023	20.5	29.0		
3	Celine Kale	6/21/2023	15.0	18.5		
4	Mark John	6/20/2023	17.5	29.5		
5	Abidah Ali	6/20/2023	10.0	25.0		

1   State the data type that is best suited for the data in each of the following fields.

Choose from the options in these boxes: (number)   (text)   (date)

  a   Name of Student

  b   Date Test Taken

  c   Math Mark

  d   Science Mark

2   The teacher enters the data 'Alex' in the Math Mark column, but she gets an error message. Explain why she got an error message.

	A	B	C	D	E
1	Name of Student ▾	Date Test Taken ▾	Math Mark ▾	Science Mar ▾	Total ▾
2	Judy Andrews	6/21/2023	20.5	29.0	
3	Celine Kale	6/21/2023	15.0	18.5	
4	Mark John	6/20/2023	17.5	29.5	
5	Abidah Ali	6/20/2023	Alex	25.0	
6					
7					
8					
9					
10					

Microsoft Excel   ✕

  ⊗   This value doesn't match the data validation restrictions defined for this cell.

                                        Retry   Cancel   Help

3   Choose the correct formula to calculate the total of the Science and Math marks for Judy Andrews in the spreadsheet.

  A   =C2+D2

  B   C2+D2=

  C   C2+D2

  D   C2+E2

4   What is the name of the function that can be used to calculate the Total Score?

   A   AVERAGE

   B   SUM

   C   +

5   To get the Total Mark for Abidah Ali, the teacher used the formula =C5+D5 instead of =10.0+25.0. Explain why.

6   Enter the data in a spreadsheet as seen below:

E6   ▼   ⋮   ✕ ✓ *fx*

	A	B	C	D
1	Name of Student	Date Test Taken	Math Mark	Science Mark
2	Judy Andrews	6/21/2023	20.5	29.0
3	Celine Kale	6/21/2023	15.0	18.5
4	Mark John	6/20/2023	17.5	29.5
5	Abidah Ali	6/20/2023	10.0	25.0

> Refer to the **Learn** panel if you need help with the steps.

Use a filter to find the records based on the criteria below:

  a   Criterion: Name of student is Mark John

  b   Criterion: Math Mark is greater than 15.0.

Did you know?

You can use the **Fill Handle** option in a spreadsheet to easily copy a formula to a series of cells. Using the Fill Handle option is faster than having to type the same formula over and over again in other cells.

E2   ▼   ⋮ ✕ ✓ *fx* =C2*D2

	A	B	C	D	E	F
1	Type of pizza	Size of pizza	Cost of pizza	Number ordered	Total Cost of pizza	
2	Garden	medium	$ 35.00	1	$35.00	
3	Cheese	medium	$ 40.00	2		
4	Tropical	large	$ 55.00	1		
5	Garden	small	$ 25.00	2		
6	Garden	large	$ 50.00	3		
7	Cheese	large	$ 50.00	7		
8	Cheese	medium	$ 40.00	4		
9						
10						
11						

Fill Handle

Challenge yourself!

Work in small groups.

Use the spreadsheet to answer the following questions.

	A	B	C	D
1	Dessert	Amount in Store	Amount Sold	Amount Remaining
2	Chocolate cake	10	4	
3	Strawberry cupcakes	48	28	
4	Blueberry muffins	72	50	
5	Scones	50	25	
6				
7	Average Amount Sold			
8	Total Amount Remaining			

1 Choose the correct formula to calculate the **number of scones remaining**.

A =B2–C2

B =B5–C5

C =B5+C5

D =B5*C5

2 Choose the correct function to calculate the **average amount of desserts sold**.

A =(C2+C3+C4+C5)/5

B =SUM(C2:C5)

C =AVERAGE(C2:C5)

D =AVERAGE(B2:B5)

3 Choose the correct function to calculate the **Total amount of desserts remaining**.

A =D2+D3+D4+D5

B =SUM(D2:D5)

C =AVERAGE(D2:D5)

D =D2-D5

4 The **Amount Sold** for chocolate cake was changed from 4 to 6. What cell values will be affected by the change?

A Total Amount Remaining

B Average Amount Sold

C Amount Remaining

5 What data type should the data in the **Dessert** fields be?

A Text

B Number

C Date

6 The data type of **Amount Sold** is Number. If text is entered in this column, what will happen?

A Error message

B Nothing will happen

Copy the table on '**Desserts**' to a spreadsheet. Complete the table with the calculations above to see if your answers are correct.

7 Use a filter to find the records with the data that meet the following criteria:

a Criterion: Blueberry muffins

b Criterion: Amount sold is greater than 25.

My project

Work in groups to complete the project.

Answer the following questions:

1 What should the data type of the values in these fields be?

	A	B	C	D	E
1	Swim Team	Date of competition	Number of competitors	Fee for each competitor	Total fees
2	Aquafins	5/7/2022	12	$15.00	
3	Dolphins	5/5/2022	10	$10.00	
4	Mermaids	5/5/2022	8	$10.00	
5	Atlantis	5/6/2022	12	$15.00	
6		Total number of competitors			
7		Average number of competitors			

   a Swim Team

   b Date of competition

   c Number of competitors

2 a Text can be entered in the Number of competitors column.

      ❏ True   ❏ False

   b Give a reason for your answer.

3 What is the formula to calculate the total fees paid by Aquafins?

   A =C2+D2

   B =C2*D2

   C =C2/D2

4 What feature can be used to copy the formula to the other cells?

   A Filter

   B Fill Handle

5 An advantage of a spreadsheet is that formulas automatically update. Explain what this means, using an example from the Swim Teams spreadsheet.

6 a Write the function to calculate the **Total number of competitors**.

   b Write the function to calculate the **Average number of competitors**.

7 Copy the Swim Teams data into a spreadsheet. Complete the table with the calculations above to see if your answers are correct.

8 Use a filter to find the records with the data that meets the following criteria.

   a Criterion: Fee is $15.00

   b Criterion: Number of competitors is greater than or equal to 8.

What can you do?

Read and review what you can do.

✔ I know about limiting cells to specific data types.

✔ I know how to create and use simple formula and functions.

✔ I know about using cell references if data might change.

✔ I know how to find data according to a criterion.

Well done! You now know about data types, formulae, functions and how to find data.

Selection

Get started!

We use conditions to make everyday choices. There are situations where we choose between two decisions based on what we observe or know to be true.

For example:

If it is my birthday, then I will eat birthday cake, otherwise I will eat a sandwich.

In Unit 6, you made a decision based on each scenario being true. Now, tell your partner what alternative decision you would make for each scenario below:

If my tablet battery is low, then I will charge it, otherwise I will _____.

If it is raining outside, then I will use an umbrella, otherwise I will _____.

If the alarm clock rings, then it is time to get up, otherwise _____.

If I am tired, then I will go to sleep, otherwise I will _____.

If the school bell rings, then it is time for class, otherwise _____.

If Cliff is thirsty, then he drinks water, otherwise he will drink juice.

You will learn to:

- understand and use If, Then, Else statements in algorithms
- understand and use the 'equal to' operator in algorithms
- develop programs with If, Then, Else statements
- develop programs using the 'equal to' operator
- develop programs for the micro:bit to produce different outputs.

In this unit, you will create programs with If…Then…Else statements in micro:bit.

Warm up

Follow the decision tree by answering the different questions. The decision tree will help choose a pet that is right for you.

```
                    Yes              Do you want a pet?              No
        ┌────────────────────────                          ────────────────────┐
        ↓                                                                       │
  Are you going to take                              No                         │
    care of your pet?  ──────────────────────────────────────────┐             │
        │                                                         │             │
       Yes                                                        │             │
        ↓                                                         │             │
  Do you want a pet      No      Do you want a pet                │             │
  you can play with?  ────────→    that can sing?                 │             │
        │                              │                          │             │
       Yes                           Yes     No                   │             │
        ↓                             ↓       ↓                   │             │
  Do you want to train                                            │             │
  your pet to do things?                                          │             │
      │          │                                                │             │
     Yes        No                                                │             │
      ↓          ↓                    ↓       ↓                    ↓             ↓
    ┌─────┐  ┌────────┐          ┌──────┐  ┌──────┐          ┌────────────────────┐
    │ Cat │  │ Rabbit │          │ Bird │  │ Fish │          │    Toy animal      │
    └─────┘  └────────┘          └──────┘  └──────┘          └────────────────────┘
```

Do you remember?

Before starting this unit, check that you can:

- use variables in algorithms
- develop programs with a variable
- understand algorithms that contain selection
- predict the outcomes of conditions within a program.

There is an online chapter all about **MakeCode for micro:bit**.

If Then Else Statements

Learn

We covered **If ... Then** selection statements in Unit 6. Now, we will be looking at another type of selection statement, the **If ... Then ... Else** statement.

The three parts of this statement are:

1   Condition (after "If")
2   Decision 1 (after "Then")
3   Decision 2 (after "Else")

Decision 1 (the '**Then**' part of the statement) is **only** carried out if the condition is **TRUE**.

However, Decision 2 (the '**Else**' part of the statement) is **only** carried out if the condition is **FALSE**.

For example,

If the weather is sunny today, **then** I will go to football practice, **else** I will stay home.

Condition   Decision 1   Decision 2

First, we check the weather today. Based on the answer we do one of two things:

1   If the condition is **true** (it is sunny), we will go to football practice
2   If the condition is **false** (it is not sunny), we will stay home.

Algorithms with the If ... Then ... Else statement

Algorithm 1	
Step	**Instruction**
①	Start program when simulator is started
②	Clear screen
③	**3.1** If logo is pressed, then
	3.1.1 Show string 'Hello!'
	3.2 Else
	3.2.1 Show heart icon
④	Repeat steps 2 and 3 forever
⑤	Stop program

Algorithm 1 begins when the simulator is started. It indefinitely checks to see when the condition is met.

The condition is: the micro:bit logo is pressed.

If condition is **true**: the word Hello! will be shown across the screen.

If condition is **false**: the heart icon will be shown on the screen.

Practise

1 Look at the following **If… Then… Else** statements and identify the following:
   - the condition
   - the outcome when the condition is **true**
   - the outcome when the condition is **false**.
   a   If the weather is cold outside, then I will wear a sweater, else I will wear a T-shirt.
   b   If the traffic light is red, then stop the vehicle, else continue driving.
   c   If it is raining, then do not water the plants, else go and water the plants.
   d   If I have exams tomorrow, then I will study, else I will go outside to play.
   e   If my pet is dirty, then I will give him a bath, else I will not bath him.

2 From Algorithm 2, identify:
   - the condition
   - the outcome when the condition is **true**
   - the outcome when the condition is **false**.

Algorithm 2	
Step	**Instruction**
①	Start program when simulator is started
②	Clear screen
③	**3.1** If Button B is pressed, then
	3.1.1 Show string 'Goodbye!'
	3.2 Else
	3.2.1 Show string "Press B"
④	Repeat steps 2 and 3 forever
⑤	Stop program

3 Fill in the blanks for Algorithm 3 using the following information:
Algorithm 3 begins when the simulator is started. It indefinitely checks to see if the condition is met.

The **condition** is: the micro:bit is shaken.

If condition is **true**: the giggle sound is played until it is done.

If condition is **false**: the happy icon will be shown on the screen.

Algorithm 3	
Step	**Instruction**
①	Start program when _____
②	**2.1** If _____, then
	2.1.1 _____
	2.2 Else
	2.2.1 _____
③	Repeat step _____ forever
④	Stop program

Algorithms with comparison

In programming, comparison operators control the flow of a program. These operators are used to compare two values in a conditional statement and give a result of either true or false.

For example, in an **If … Then … Else** statement, a comparison operator tells the program to execute different sections of code based on whether the result is true or false.

There are six comparison operators:

Operator Name	Operator Symbol
Equal to	=
Not equal to	≠
Greater than	>
Greater than or equal to	≥
Less than	<
Less than or equal to	≤

Equal to Operator

We will be looking at the equal to = operator in this unit. The equal to operator compares two values. These values can be numbers, text or variables.

The equal to operator gives a result that is **true** if the value on the left is equal to the value on the right. Otherwise, it gives a result that is false.

In micro:bit, the equal to block is found in the **Logic** group under the **Comparison** section.

Algorithms with an Equal to Operator – Algorithm 4

Step	Instruction
1	Start program when micro:bit is shaken
2	Create variable called Animal
3	Set Animal to randomly pick a number from 1 to 2
4	**4.1** If Animal = 1, then
	4.1.1 Show Giraffe icon
	4.2 Else
	4.2.1 Show Duck icon
5	Stop program

The algorithm begins when the shake button is clicked on the simulator.

The variable, **Animal**, is set to randomly pick the number 1 or 2.

The condition is: the variable, Animal, is equal to 1.

If condition is **true**: the Giraffe icon will be shown on the screen.

If condition is **false**: the Duck icon will be shown on the screen.

Each time the micro:bit is shaken, the variable, Animal, will choose a number, either 1 or 2.

We will learn more about creating variables in the next section.

Practise

1   Determine if the following is true or false:

   a   8 = 8

   b
   =

   c   10 = 15

   d

2   Algorithm for a Night light

Algorithm 5	
Step	**Instruction**
①	Start program when Button A is pressed
②	Create variable called Light
③	Set Light to randomly pick a whole number from 0 to 5
④	**4.1** If Light = 5, then
	4.1.1 Show all LEDs lighting
	4.2 Else
	4.2.1 Clear screen
⑤	Stop program

From the Algorithm, identify the following:

   a   The input to the program

   b   The variable

   c   The condition

   d   The outcome if the condition is true

   e   The outcome if the condition is false.

We will show how to pick random numbers in the next section.

Programs with If ... Then ... Else Statements

Creating programs with If ... Then ... Else statement
We will use Microsoft MakeCode for micro:bit to create the program for Algorithm 4 on page 108.

1   Create a new project named **Algorithm 4**.

2   Delete the **on start** and **forever** blocks from the programming area.

3   Go to the **Input** group. Add the **on shake** block to the programming area.

4   Go to the **Variables** group. Click on **Make a variable**. Type 'Animal' and select ok.

5   From the **Variables** group, add the **set (variable) to** block.

6   From the **Math** group, add the **pick random** block inside of the **set Animal to** block. Change the number 0 to 1 and the number 10 to 2.

7   From the **Logic** group, add the **if ... then ... else** block.

8   From the **Logic** group, add the **equal to** block inside the **if ... then ... else** block.

9   From the **Variables** group, add the **Animal** variable to the first part of the **equal to** block. Change the number from **0** to **1** in the second part of the **equal to** block.

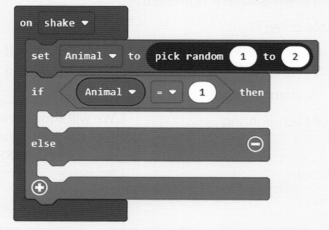

10　Go to the **Basic** group. Add the **show icon** block after the **if ... then** statement. Click the drop-down arrow. Select the **Giraffe** icon.

11　Go to the **Basic** group. Add the **show icon** block after the **else** statement. Click the drop-down arrow. Select the **Duck** icon.

The final code is:

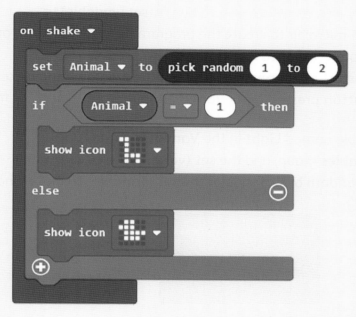

12　Click **play** to start the simulator. You will see the **shake** button appear on the micro:bit.

13　Click on the **shake** button to run the program.

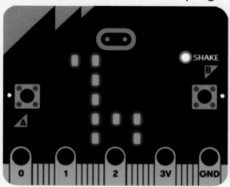 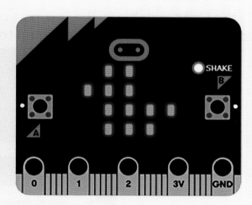

A Giraffe icon will appear on the screen when the variable Animal equals to number 1. A Duck icon will appear on the screen when the variable Animal chooses number 2.

14　Save your project.

Practise

1 Which groups do the following blocks belong to in MakeCode for micro:bit?
   a equal to   b if … then … else
   c on shake   d show icon
   e pick random   f set (variable) to

2 Use MakeCode for micro:bit to create the program for the Night light on page 109.
   a Create a new project named Algorithm 5.
   b Delete the **on start** and **forever** blocks from the programming area.
   c Add the **on button pressed** block from the Input group. Select 'A' from the drop-down arrow.
   d Create a variable named **Light** in the **Variables** group.
   e From the **Variables** group, add the **set (variable) to** block.
   f Add the **pick random** block inside of the **set (variable) to** block. Change the number 10 to 5.

   g Add the **if … then … else** block.
   h Add the **equal to** block inside the **if … then … else** block.
   i Add the **Light** variable to the first part of the **equal to** block. Change the number from 0 to **5** in the second part of the **equal to** block.

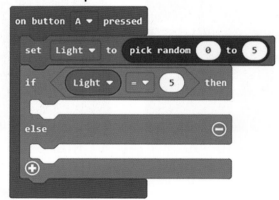

   j Go to the **Basic** group. Add the **show leds** block after the **if … then** statement. Click on all 25 leds to light them up.
   k Go to the **Basic** group. Add the **clear screen** block after the **else** statement.
   l Click **play** to start the simulator.
   m Click on button A to run the program. Save your project.

Go further

1   Look at the **Algorithm for the Thermometer**. Identify the following:
   a   The input for the program
   b   The condition
   c   The outcome when the condition is true
   d   The outcome when the condition is false.

   Algorithm for Thermometer

Step	Instruction
❶	Start program when button B is pressed
❷	Show number temperature (°C)
❸	Create variable called Right Temp
❹	Set Right Temp to 25
❺	Clear screen
❻	**6.1** If temperature (°C) = Right Temp, then
	6.1.1 Show string "Right temperature"
	6.2 Else
	6.2.1 Show string "Wrong temperature"
❼	Stop program

Remember: The micro:bit has a built-in temperature sensor that measures how hot or cold the environment is.

2   Use MakeCode for micro:bit to create the program for the Thermometer.
   a   Create a new project named Thermometer.
   b   Delete the **on start** and **forever** blocks from the programming area.
   c   Add the **on button pressed** block. Select 'B' from the drop-down arrow.
   d   From the **Basic** group, add the **show number** block.
   e   From the **Input** group, add the **temperature (°C)** block inside the **show number** block.

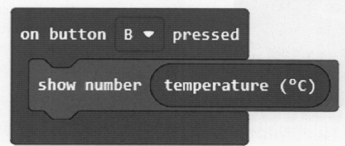

f   Create a variable named **Right Temp** in the **Variables** group.

g   Add the **set (variable) to** block. Change the number from 0 to 25.

h   Add the **clear screen** block.

i   Add the **if … then … else** block.

j   Add the **equal to** block inside the **if … then … else** block.

k   Add the **temperature (°C)** block to the first part of the **equal to** block.

l   Add the **Right Temp** variable to the second part of the **equal to** block.

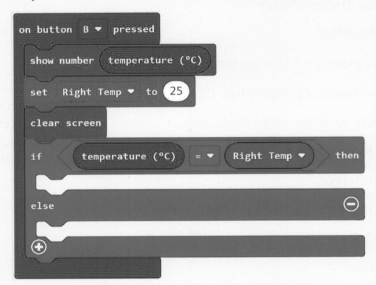

m   From the **Basic** group, add the **show string** block after the **if … then** statement. Change the word 'Hello' to 'Right temperature'.

n   Add a **show string** block after the **else** statement. Change the word 'Hello' to 'Wrong temperature'.

o   Click **play** to start the simulator.

p   Click on button B to run the program. Describe what happens on the micro:bit.

q   Click and drag the thermometer level on the simulator to read 25°C, or put the physical micro:bit in a very warm place. Describe what happens in either case.

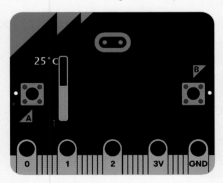

The **show number** block outputs a number to the screen. The **show string** block outputs any letter or word to the screen.

r   Save your project.

Challenge yourself!

1 Look at the Algorithm for the Decision Maker. Identify the following:
   a the input for the program
   b the condition
   c the outcome when the condition is true
   d the outcome when the condition is false.

Algorithm for Decision Maker

Step	Instruction
1	Start program when logo is touched
2	Create variable called Answer
3	Set Answer to randomly pick either true or false
4	**4.1** If Answer = true, then
	4.1.1 Show yes icon
	4.1.2 Pause for 2 seconds
	4.1.3 Clear screen
	4.2 Else
	4.2.1 Show no icon
	4.2.2 Pause for 2 seconds
	4.2.3 Clear screen
5	Stop program

2 Code the program for the Decision Maker:
   a Create a new project and name it Decision Maker.
   b Delete the **on start** and **forever** blocks from the programming area.
   c Add the **on logo** block. Select **touched** from the drop-down menu.
   d Create a variable and name it **Answer**.
   e Add the remaining blocks of code to form the program.
   f Click **play** to start the simulator.
   g Click on the logo 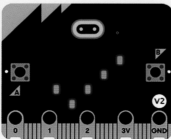 to run the program.

When the condition is **true**, you will see the following:

When the condition is **false**, you will see the following:

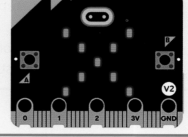

You will find:

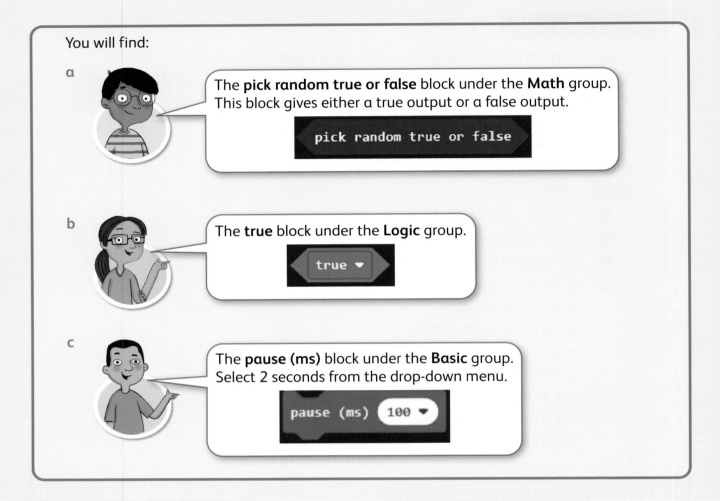

a   The **pick random true or false** block under the **Math** group.
This block gives either a true output or a false output.

```
pick random true or false
```

b   The **true** block under the **Logic** group.

```
true ▼
```

c   The **pause (ms)** block under the **Basic** group.
Select 2 seconds from the drop-down menu.

```
pause (ms)  100 ▼
```

My project

Step Counter

1   Fill in the blanks for Algorithm 7 using the following information:
  - The program begins when the micro:bit is shaken.
  - The condition is: the number of steps is equal to 10.
  - If condition is **true**:
    a   show the word 'Stop!' on the screen
    b   show the number of steps
    c   set the number of steps to 0.
  - If condition is **false**:
    a   show the word 'Go!' on the screen
    b   show the number of steps.

Algorithm 6	
Step	**Instruction**
❶	Start program when simulator is started
❷	Create variable called Steps
❸	Set Steps to 0
❹	Stop program

Algorithm 7	
Step	**Instruction**
❶	Start program when _____
❷	Change Steps by 1
❸	Clear screen
❹	**4.1** If _____ = _____, then
	4.1.1 Show string _____
	4.1.2 Show number of _____
	4.2.2 Set Steps to _____
	4.2 Else
	4.2.1 Show string _____
	4.2.2 Show number of _____
❺	Stop program

Hint: After you create a variable name steps, then the **change steps by 1** block will appear in the **Variables** group.

2   Code the program for a Step Counter:
   a   Create a new project and name it Step Counter.
   b   Delete the **forever** block from the programming area.
   c   Add the blocks of code for Algorithm 6 to the **Start** block.
   d   Add the blocks of code for Algorithm 7.
   e   Click **play** to start the simulator and run Algorithm 6.
   f   Click on the shake button to run Algorithm 7.
   g   Continue to click the shake button until the step counter reads 10.
   h   What do you observe?

Did you know?

An online quiz is programmed using the If … Then … Else condition. When the user selects an answer, the program checks to see if the correct answer was selected. If the user chose the correct answer, then the program will show a green tick next to the question. Else, the program will show a red 'x' next to the question. This means the incorrect answer was chosen.

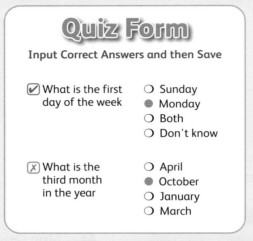

What can you do?

Read and review what you can do.

✔ I can use the If … Then … Else statement in algorithms.

✔ I can use the equal to operator in algorithms.

✔ I can create programs with If … Then … Else statements.

✔ I can develop programs using the 'equal to' operator.

✔ I can develop programs for the micro:bit to produce different outputs.

Well done! Now you can create programs with selection on micro:bit!

Network devices

Get started!

Have you used a smartphone? Tell your partner about the following.

- What different things do you do on your smartphone?
- Where do you use your smartphone?
- What are the differences between a smartphone and a house phone?

Why do think a house phone cannot be used in the park to make calls?

You will learn:

- how mobile devices connect to the internet using a cellular network
- that data is divided into packets that are reassembled at the destination
- that packets can follow different routes across the internet before being reassembled
- about issues that may occur as a result of internet failure.

In this unit, you will learn how mobile devices connect to the internet, how data travels over the internet and about issues due to internet failure.

Warm up

To complete this task, you need:

- a pair of scissors
- a plain sheet of paper
- three small envelopes.

Write the following message on a sheet of paper:

1
How are you?

2
Would you like
to play

3
football this evening?

1   Cut the message into three pieces, as shown above.

2   Place each piece of paper in a different envelope.

3   Number each envelope according to the order of the message.

4   Write the name of one student in your class on each envelope.

5   Write your name on the back of the envelope.

6   Give each envelope to a different student in your class. Each student should pass the envelope to the person next to them until it reaches the destination student.

The student receiving the three envelopes must now open the envelopes and put the pieces of the message together.

What order did the envelopes arrive in?

How did the receiving student know what order to put the message in?

Do you remember?

Before you start this unit, check that you:

- know that all devices on a network have an IP address
- know how websites are stored on servers and accessed over the internet
- can explain the role of switches, routers and Wi-Fi access points in a network.

Networks
Cellular network

Connecting to the internet anytime and anywhere is an essential part of our lives.

A Wi-Fi network only covers a small area. If you want to access the internet in any location, your mobile device must connect to a cellular network.

A cellular network is a communications network made up of overlapping cells. Each cell covers a small area of land in a hexagonal shape. Each cell contains a base station. The base station includes a cell tower with antennas.

Keywords

cellular network: a type of communication network used by mobile phones

cell: an area in a cellular network that is covered by a signal from a single base station

hexagonal: a shape that has six equal sides in length and six equal angles

antenna: a device that can broadcast and receive signals

The antennas on each cell tower are used to send and receive data wirelessly using radio waves.

The base station sends and receives data from mobile devices and connects them to the internet.

Overlapping cells provide network coverage over a large land area.

Accessing a website using a mobile device

When a user makes a request for a website or app on a mobile device, a signal is sent to the nearest cell tower.

a The antenna on the cell tower receives the request and sends it to the mobile internet service provider's (ISP) network.

b The request is sent through the internet until it reaches the correct server.

c   The server hosting the website sends the requested data back through the internet to the mobile ISP's network.

d   The ISP sends the data to the base station closest to the mobile device.

e   The data is then sent from the base station cell tower to the mobile device.

Overlapping cells keep users connected to the network. If the user moves into a new cell, the mobile device will connect to the tower in the new cell, with a stronger signal, and release the tower in the old cell with the weaker signal. This maintains the best connection at all times.

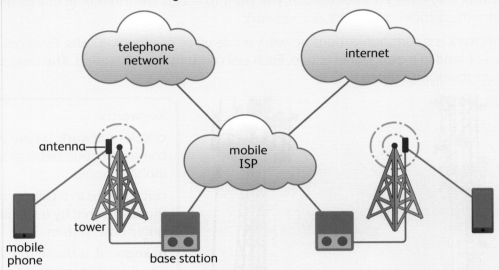

Did you know?

The first mobile phone with internet connectivity was the Nokia 9000 Communicator, which was launched in Finland in 1996.

Practise

1   State whether the following statements are true or false.
   a   Mobile phones can be used to make phone calls while on a train.
   b   Mobile devices can access the internet by using wireless signals.
   c   A cell tower has an antenna that can only receive signals from mobile phones.
   d   A cell is a place where mobile phones are stored.
   e   A cell tower uses Wi-Fi to connect to mobile devices.

2   Tell your partner what a cell in a cellular network is.

3   Tell your partner what equipment is found at a cell site.

4   What happens when a mobile device requests data from a website? Explain all of the steps to your partner.

5   How can a mobile device continue to access the internet while travelling in a car over a long distance?

Data packets

Data that is sent over a network is broken into smaller pieces of data known as **data packets**.

Every web page you look at, or email you receive, travels across the internet in lots of separate data packets.

Every email or file you send over the internet is also broken down into lots of separate data packets.

Each packet that is sent over the internet includes the following:

- **The sender's IP address:** this is the IP address of the device sending the data.
- **The receiver's IP address:** this is the IP address of the device being sent the data. This is so data can be sent to the right place.
- **The sequence of the packets:** each data packet is numbered in order. This is so the data can be reassembled exactly as it was before it was sent.
- **The payload:** the payload is the actual data being sent (for example, the contents of an email). This is usually the largest part of the packet.

Packet-Email Example

Header	Sender's IP address Receiver's IP address The sequence number of the packets Number of packets
Payload	Data

Data packets travel from one router to another across the internet.

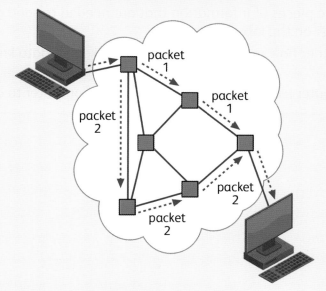

When a packet arrives at a router, the router looks at the receiver's IP address:

- it checks to see if that address is connected to its own network
- if not, the packet is sent on to another router on another network.

Eventually, after passing through several networks and routers, the packet will come to a router that is connected to a device with the correct IP address. This router will forward the packet to this device.

Related data packets do not usually follow the same path. Instead, they are each sent using the best route available at that moment in time. This speeds up the sending of data over a network and makes it more efficient.

As the packets arrive at their destination, the receiving computer assembles the data packets in the correct order. This recreates the original data that was sent.

Keywords

data packets: small pieces of data that are sent over the internet

payload: the data transported by a packet

Practise

1 State whether the following statements are true or false.
   a An email is usually sent as one complete message.
   b Routers help to get a message from one computer to another over the internet.
   c Data is broken into smaller pieces and sent over the internet as packets.
   d Sending data in packets slows down the internet.
   e All data packets that make up the same email are sent along the same route to the destination computer.

2 Explain to your partner why a file is broken into smaller pieces of data before being sent to a destination computer over the internet.

3 Tell your friend three pieces of information that are needed to send a message from one computer to another on the internet.

4 Explain to your partner how a computer receiving packets of data knows how to put the data back together.

5 What role does a router play in sending data from one computer to another?

Internet failure

In many places around the world, the internet has become an important part of everyday life. Many people and businesses rely on the internet for their day-to-day activities. Any disruptions to the internet can affect many people in different ways.

For example, internet failure at the bank would mean:

- Payments by bank cards at supermarkets and other businesses would no longer be possible.
- ATMs would not connect to the bank's servers and would not be able to give out cash.
- Without access to cash, people would not be able to buy groceries or pay for gas at the gas station.

Many companies and institutions store data and software in the cloud. Internet failure would stop their access.

- Doctors might not be able to access patient data that is essential to saving someone's life.
- The police might not be able to check the identities of criminals.

The transport system would also be affected as airlines, buses and trains use online ticketing systems. Without the internet, travellers would not be able to:

- purchase tickets online
- pay for tickets using bank cards
- have tickets checked electronically.

Failure of the internet would affect many activities at schools. For example,

- schools would not be able to conduct online classes.
- students could not send emails, messages or documents to teachers and classmates.

Without the internet, online entertainment sites could not provide their services. This would mean:

- you would not be able to watch your favourite shows
- you would not be able to play online games with your friends.

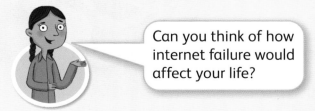

Can you think of how internet failure would affect your life?

Did you know?

Damage to fibre optic cables deep underwater, which provide internet services to many countries, is a major cause of internet failure.

An autonomous underwater vehicle (AUV) rover-drone inspects a submarine internet communication cable on the seabed in the ocean.

Practise

1 Tell your partner what internet failure is.
2 Tell your partner some of the things you would not be able to do if the internet was not working.
3 Tell your partner how internet failure would affect some of your school activities.
4 State one way that internet failure can affect the business of a supermarket.
5 Tell your partner how internet failure may affect the operations of a bank.
6 Tell your partner how internet failure may affect the duties of the police.

Go further

1 Tell your classmate how a mobile device is able to access the internet.
2 Using an example, explain how data travels from one computer to another over the internet.
3 What happens to packets of data when they arrive at the destination computer?
4 Tell your classmate how customers at a supermarket may be affected if there is no internet service.

Challenge yourself!

1 Tell your partner how a mobile device in a car can keep its connection to the internet while moving.
2 Explain the role of a router in transporting a file from one computer to another over the internet.
3 Explain to your partner how you think a hospital may be affected if there is no internet access.
4 Discuss with your partner how stocking the shelves of a supermarket might be affected if there is an internet failure.
5 Write what services in a library might be affected if there is an internet failure.

My project

1 Draw:
   a a picture of a cell site
   b an overhead diagram of seven overlapping cells.
2 Draw a diagram to show what happens when someone makes a request for a website using their mobile device.
3 You get up one morning and realise that the internet is not working. You hear on the news that there would be no internet access for a few days. Write a short letter to your friend explaining some of the difficulties you and your family would encounter during the days without internet access.

What can you do?

Read and review what you can do.

✔ I can explain how mobile devices use a cellular network to access the internet.

✔ I know what a data packet is.

✔ I can describe how data is sent from one computer to another over the internet.

✔ I can identify issues that may occur as a result of internet failure.

Well done! Now you know about cellular networks and data packets!

Be a game developer

Creating games

Get started!

In groups of three, discuss how variables could be used in the real world, such as in:

a computer games

b supermarkets

You will learn to:

- use addition and subtraction in algorithms
- change variables using addition and subtraction operators
- evaluate programs against given criteria.

In this unit, you will develop algorithms and programs in Scratch with arithmetic operators.

Warm up

Work in pairs. Using the directions below, instruct the robot vacuum cleaner to collect the coins while avoiding the obstacles marked as "X".

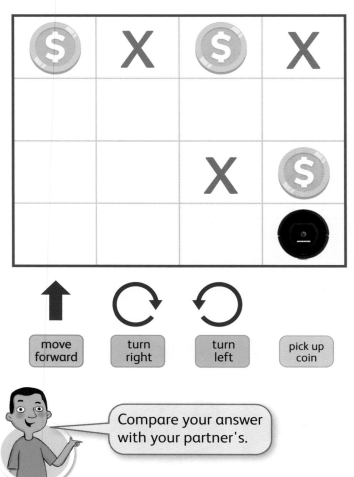

move forward   turn right   turn left   pick up coin

Compare your answer with your partner's.

Step	Instruction
1	↑
2	
3	
4	
5	
6	
7	
8	
9	
10	
11	
12	
13	
14	

Do you remember?

Before you start this unit, check that you:
- can use variables in algorithms
- know how to develop programs with a variable assigned to a specific value
- can use selection in algorithms: IF, THEN, ELSE
- can develop programs with simple conditional or selection statements, including IF, THEN, ELSE, to produce different outputs.

In this unit, you will use Scratch. There is an online chapter all about Scratch.

Arithmetic operators

Arithmetic operators such as addition (+) and subtraction (–) can be used to perform calculations in an algorithm. Calculations can involve constants or variables. The results can also be stored as a variable.

Consider the following two problems:

Problem 1

Write an algorithm to:

- ask a user to enter two numbers
- output the total of the two numbers.

The algorithm can be written as follows:

Input A (First number)
Input B (Second Number)
Let Total = A + B
Output Total

> **Keyword**
>
> **operator:** a character or symbol that tells us what action is to be performed

When a user enters the numbers, they are stored in the variables **A** and **B**. The algorithm adds the values stored in these variables together. The answer is stored in the variable **Total**.

Each time we work through the algorithm, the user can store different values in the variables A and B.

5		10		15
A		B		Total

Problem 2

Write an algorithm to:

- ask a user to enter two numbers and
- subtract the second number from the first.

The algorithm can be written as follows:

Input A (First number)
Input B (Second number)
Let Answer = A – B
Output Answer

> Let's look at another example of the use of the addition (+) and subtraction (–) operators.

When the user enters the numbers, they are stored in the variables **A** and **B**. The algorithm subtracts the values stored in these two variables. The answer is stored in the variable **Answer**.

Algorithm for quiz game

In this example, we want to create an algorithm for the **Penguin** Sprite. When the Green Flag is clicked, the **Penguin** should ask a question and the user should be able to type an answer.

The user starts with 20 points. If the answer to a question is correct, the user gains 10 points. If the answer is wrong, the user loses 5 points.

The table below shows the complete algorithm that uses variables and the addition and subtraction operators.

Step	Instruction
1	Start program when the Green Flag is clicked
2	Create a variable called Points
3	Create a variable called Answer
4	Set variable Points to 20 ← Points = 20
5	Set variable Answer to " " ← Answer = " "
6	Ask "What is the capital city of China?" and wait
7	Set variable Answer to text entered in Step 6 ← Answer = "Beijing"
8	**8.1** If Answer = "Beijing", then: **8.1.1** Set variable Points = Points + 10 ← Points = 30 **8.1.2** Say "Correct" for 2 seconds **8.2** Else: **8.2.1** Set variable Points = Points – 5 **8.1.2** Say "Wrong" for 2 seconds
9	End program

The boxes show the values for the variables if the user enters the correct answer.

What value would be stored in the variable **Points** if the answer is wrong?

In Step 5, we set the Answer variable to " ". This is because some programming languages need each variable to be given an initial value. In this case, the initial value is a blank space.

Practise

1   Write an algorithm that asks a user to input three numbers and find the total of the three numbers.

2   A customer has 100 dollars and buys two items in a supermarket. Write an algorithm to ask a user to enter the cost of each item and output the change the user will get.

3   Write a new algorithm for the **Penguin** Sprite. When the sprite is clicked, the **Penguin** should ask **two** questions. The user should be able to type an answer for each question. The user starts with 25 points. If the answer to a question is correct, the user gains 10 points. If the answer is wrong, the user loses 5 points.

Complete the table below for this algorithm by choosing the correct words, numbers or symbols at the bottom of this page.

Step	Instruction
1	Start program when this _____ is clicked
2	Create variable called Points
3	Create variable called Answer
4	Set variable Points to _____
5	Set variable Answer to " "
6	_____ "What is the capital city of India?" and wait
7	Set variable Answer to text entered in Step _____
8	**8.1** If Answer = "New Delhi", then: **8.1.1** Set variable Points = Points + 10 **8.1.2** Say "_____" for 2 seconds **8.2** Else: **8.2.1** Set variable Points = _____ – 5 **8.2.2** Say "Wrong" for 2 seconds
9	Ask "What is the capital city of Spain?" and wait
10	Set variable Answer to text entered in Step 9
11	**11.1** If _____ = "Madrid", then: **11.1.1** Set variable Points = Points _____ 10 **11.1.2** Say "Correct" for 2 seconds **11.2** Else: **11.2.1** Set variable Points = Points _____ 5 **11.2.2** Say "Wrong" for 2 seconds
12	End program

Hint: Use each word only once.

What is the capital city of India?

a	Correct	b	25	c	6
d	+	e	sprite	f	Answer
g	ask	h	Points	i	–

Adding and subtracting variables

Learn

We will create a program with variables for the quiz game algorithm in the last **Learn** panel. It will add and subtract numbers the user enters.

Program for quiz game

When the Green Flag is clicked, the **Penguin** asks a question and the user is able to type an answer. The user starts with 20 points. If the answer to a question is correct, the user gains 10 points. If the answer is wrong, the user loses 5 points. We can follow the steps below to create the program:

1 Open a new project in Scratch.

2 Add the **Artic** Backdrop to your project.

3 Add the **Penguin 2** Sprite to your project.

4 Create a variable called **Points**.

5 Add the code below to **Penguin 2**.

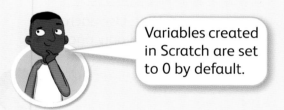

Variables created in Scratch are set to 0 by default.

The complete program uses a variable, and the addition and subtraction operators.

You should notice that this program matches the algorithm. However, we did not code the following instructions:

- Step 3: Create variable called Answer
- Step 5: Set variable Answer to " "
- Step 7: Set variable Answer to text entered in Step 4

This is because in Scratch there is an **Ask and wait** coding block. It has a built-in variable called **answer** that stores whatever the user enters.

You can access the Equal to comparison **operator**, the **Addition** math operator and the **Subtraction** math operator from the **Operators** group of blocks.

Coding blocks for different variables can be inserted in these green Operator coding blocks.

Keyword

comparison operator: when the = sign is used to check if one value is the same as another, it is called a comparison operator

Variables and calculations

Variables can be used to store the score in a game, keep a count of something or store the value of calculations.

Look at the formula below to calculate the perimeter of the triangle shown. The perimeter (P) is the distance around a shape.

$P = a + b + c$

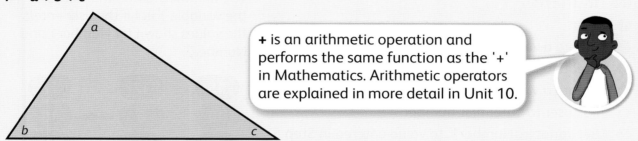

+ is an arithmetic operation and performs the same function as the '+' in Mathematics. Arithmetic operators are explained in more detail in Unit 10.

A program or algorithm can calculate the perimeter of a triangle using this formula. The user can enter different values for sides a, b and c. The perimeter of a triangle is calculated by adding the three sides. a, b and c are variables as they can change for each calculation. There are no constants in this formula.

If the user enters 10 for **side a** when the program first runs, this means that the variable a holds the value 10. If the user then enters 6 for **side b**, this means the variable b holds the value 6. If the user then enters 4 for **side c**, this means the variable c holds the value 4.

The computer uses these values to calculate the perimeter, which will be 10 + 6 + 4 = 20. The variable P holds the value 20. The algorithm or program then ends.

When the algorithm or program is run again, the user enters new values for the 3 sides. The variables a, b and c will hold these new values. The variable P will hold the new result.

Each time the program is executed, the values in the variables can change. Here we can see that we can store different values for the variables.

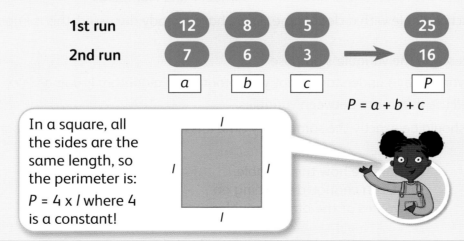

	a	b	c		P
1st run	12	8	5		25
2nd run	7	6	3	→	16

$P = a + b + c$

In a square, all the sides are the same length, so the perimeter is:

$P = 4 \times l$ where 4 is a constant!

135

Variables allow us to store and change data as an algorithm or program runs.

Example of an algorithm with variables

To create an algorithm that adds two numbers, we need three variables:

1   **Number1** – is assigned to the first number the user enters
2   **Number2** – is assigned to the second number the user enters
3   **Total** – is assigned to the result when the numbers are added.

The algorithm is:

Step	Instruction
①	Start
②	Create a variable called Number1
③	Create a variable called Number2
④	Create a variable called Total
⑤	Ask user to enter first number
⑥	Set variable, Number1, to value entered in Step 5
⑦	Ask user to enter second number
⑧	Set variable, Number2, to value entered in Step 7
⑨	Add Number1 and Number2
⑩	Set variable, Total, to value calculated in Step 9
⑪	Display the value of the variable Total
⑫	End

The following shows the values of the variable Total if the user enters the values shown for Number1 and Number2.

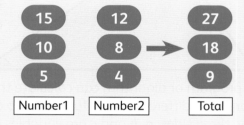

| Number1 | Number2 | Total |

The following shows the values of the variable Total if the user enters the values shown for Number1 and Number2.

You should notice that each variable is assigned.

*   The Number1 variable is assigned to the user's first input.
*   Number2 is assigned to the user's second input.
*   Total is assigned to the result of the addition of Number1 and Number2.

We also created each variable with a clear name. As we have already discussed, this is important so that:

*   they correctly describe the variable's purpose
*   it is easy for anyone else to understand what your program or algorithm is doing
*   we can easily tell the difference between variables.

A variable's name should be exactly the same every time it is used in an algorithm or program.

We can see how the variable, Total, can change depending on the values of the other variables.

Practise

1   Create a new program for the **Penguin** Sprite to do the following:
   - When the space key is pressed, the **Penguin** should ask two questions and the user should be able to type an answer for each question.
   - The user starts with 30 points.
   - If the answer to a question is correct, the user gains 10 points.
   - If the answer is wrong, the user loses 5 points.

2   Use all the coding blocks shown below in your program.

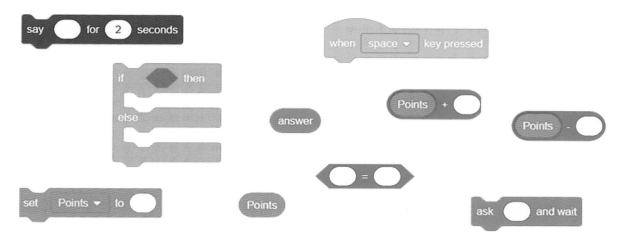

3   Run and test your program to check that you get the correct results.

Hint: Some coding blocks shown are used more than once.
Compare your solution to your partner's.

4   Write an algorithm that adds together three numbers entered by the user. Complete the table below. This algorithm has four variables.

Step	Instruction
1	Create a variable _____
2	Create a variable _____
3	Create a variable _____
4	Create a variable _____
5	Ask user to enter first number
6	Set variable, _____, to value entered in Step 1
7	Ask user to enter second number
8	Set variable, _____, to value entered in Step 2
9	Ask user to enter _____ number
10	Set variable, _____, to value entered in Step ____
11	Add _____
12	Set _____
13	Display _____

Hint: You could name your four variables:
- Number1
- Number2
- Number3
- Total

Evaluating programs

Learn

We evaluate programs against criteria. The criteria are the results we need.

It is essential to test sections of code, and the entire program, to make sure they run correctly.

We evaluate the algorithm first, to make sure it is correct.

Then we evaluate the code to make sure it matches each line in the algorithm.

Example of evaluating a program

In this example, we want to create a Pong game in Scratch. The criteria for this program are:

The correct algorithm for this program is shown in the tables below.

1   The ball should move around the stage.

2   The user should be able to control a paddle by moving the mouse pointer.

3   The ball should bounce off the paddle.

Evaluation: The code on the right matches each line in the algorithm and satisfies each criterion.

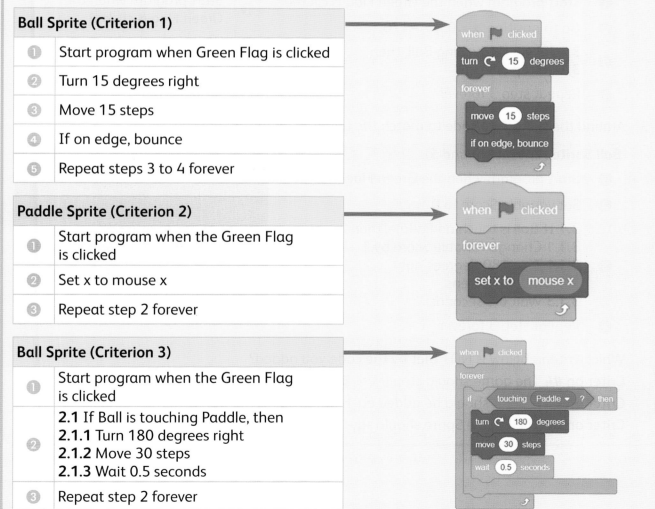

Ball Sprite (Criterion 1)	
①	Start program when Green Flag is clicked
②	Turn 15 degrees right
③	Move 15 steps
④	If on edge, bounce
⑤	Repeat steps 3 to 4 forever

Paddle Sprite (Criterion 2)	
①	Start program when the Green Flag is clicked
②	Set x to mouse x
③	Repeat step 2 forever

Ball Sprite (Criterion 3)	
①	Start program when the Green Flag is clicked
②	2.1 If Ball is touching Paddle, then 2.1.1 Turn 180 degrees right 2.1.2 Move 30 steps 2.1.3 Wait 0.5 seconds
③	Repeat step 2 forever

Practise

A. Create the Pong game from the **Learn** panel as follows:

1 Open a new project in Scratch.

2 Add the **Neon Tunnel** Backdrop.

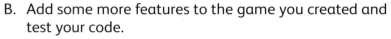
Ball   Paddle

3 Search and select the **Ball** and **Paddle** Sprites.

4 Add all the code on the previous page to your sprites.

5 Run your program and check that you get the required results.

Does your program meet Criteria 1, 2 and 3?

B. Add some more features to the game you created and test your code.

1 Add and position the **Line** Sprite close to the bottom of the stage.

2 Add code to these two sprites to match the algorithms below.

Line Sprite (Criterion 4)	
❶	Start program when the Green Flag is clicked
❷	Go to position: x = 0, y = −170
❸	**3.1** If Line is touching Ball, then **3.1.1** Stop all code
❹	Repeat step 3 forever

Paddle Sprite (Criterion 6)	
❶	Start program when the Green Flag is clicked
❷	Wait until variable Score = 5
❸	Say "You Win!"
❹	Stop all code

3 Amend the Ball Sprite code to match the updated algorithm below.

Ball Sprite (Criterion 3 and 5)	
❶	Start program when the Green Flag is clicked
❷	Set variable Score to 0
❸	**3.1 If** Ball is touching Paddle, then **3.1.1** Change variable Score by 1 **3.1.1** Turn 180 degrees right **3.1.2** Move 30 steps **3.1.3** Wait 0.5 seconds
❹	Repeat step 3 forever

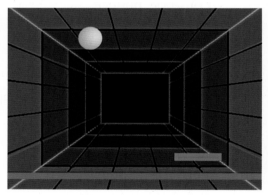

4 Which criteria below is NOT met by the code you added?

Criterion #4 The game should stop if the **Ball** hits a red line.

Criterion #5 A point should be added each time you hit the **Ball** with the **Paddle**.

Criterion #6 The Paddle Sprite should say "You Win!" when you score 10 points.

Go further

Computational thinking

Complete the instructions for an algorithm that adds two numbers, 4 and 6.

Step	Instruction
1	Start program when the Green Flag is clicked
2	Create variable called Number1
3	Create variable called Number2
4	Create variable called Answer
5	Set variable _____
6	Set variable _____
7	Set variable _____ = Number1 _____

1 Open a new project and add the **Chalkboard** Backdrop.

2 Add the **Avery** Sprite to your project and increase her size to the 150 setting.

3 Create a program for this sprite to match the algorithm below.

Step	Instruction
1	Start program when the Green Flag is clicked
2	Create variable called Score
3	Create variable called Answer
4	Set variable Points to 5
5	Set variable Answer to " "
6	Ask "True/False: The sun is a star?" and wait
7	Set variable Answer to text entered in step 6
8	**8.1** If Answer = "True", then: **8.1.1** Set variable Score = Score + 5 **8.1.2** Say "Correct" for 2 seconds **8.2** Else: **8.2.1** Set variable Score = Score – 5 **8.1.2** Say "Wrong" for 2 seconds

Compare your program to your partner's.

4 Run and test your program to check that you get the desired results.

5 Does the program meet the following criteria? Give reasons for your answer.

Criterion #1: When the space key is pressed, the **Avery** Sprite should ask a question and the user should be able to type an answer for the question.

Criterion #2: The points should start at 10.

Criterion #3: Add 5 points for a right answer, take away 5 points for a wrong answer.

Challenge yourself!

Make changes to your program from the **Go Further** activity.

1 Make changes to your code for the **Avery** Sprite to match the algorithm below.

Step	Instruction (New Algorithm)
❶	Start program when space key is pressed
❷	Create variable called Score
❸	Create variable called Answer
❹	Set variable Points to 10
❺	Set variable Answer to " "
❻	Ask "True/False: The sun is a star?" and wait
❼	Set variable Answer to text entered in step 6
❽	**8.1** If Answer = "False", then: **8.1.1** Set variable Score = Score – 5 **8.2** Else: **8.2.1** Set variable Score = Score + 5

Note: You can create text sprites on Scratch.

2 Check that you get the correct results and debug your code.

3 Create a new sprite by clicking the **Paint** icon. Name the sprite, **Win**.

4 Use the **Text** tool to write the message, "You Won!" You can change the font colour, size, and style of the text sprite.

5 Click the **Code** tab and add the code below to the **Win** Sprite.

6 State in your own words what this code does.

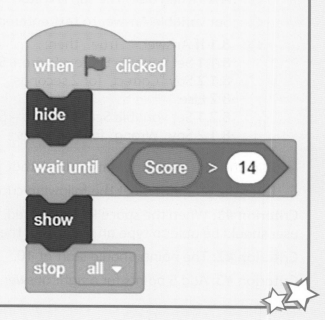

My project

1   Complete the algorithm below for a quiz game. In this game, the user should be asked two mathematics questions. They should:
   - gain 1 point for each correct answer
   - lose 1 point for each wrong answer
   - start the score at 0.

Step	Instruction (New Algorithm)
❶	Start program when the Green Flag is clicked
❷	Create variable _____
❸	Create variable _____
❹	Set variable _____
❺	Ask "What is 6 + 12?" and wait
❻	Set variable _____
❼	**7.1** If _____ = "18", then: **7.1.1** _____ **7.1.2** Say "Correct" _____ **7.2** Else: **7.2.1** _____ **7.2.2** Say "Wrong" for _____
❽	Ask "What is 20 − 16?" and wait
❾	Set variable _____
❿	**10.1** If _____ = "4", then: **10.1.1** _____ **10.1.2** Say "Correct" _____ **10.2** Else: **10.2.1** _____ **10.2.2** Say "Wrong" _____

2   Open a new project and add the **School** Backdrop.

3   Add the **Jaime** Sprite to your project.

4   Create a program for this sprite to match the algorithm for **1**.

5   Run and test your program to check that you get the correct results.

6   Does the program met the following criteria? Give reasons for your answer.

   Criterion #1: When the green flag is clicked, the sprite should ask three questions.

   Criterion #2: The user should be able to type an answer for each question.

   Criterion #3: If the answer to a question is correct, the user gains 10 points.

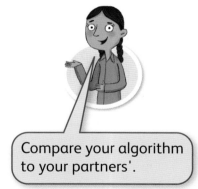

Compare your algorithm to your partners'.

7 Make the following changes to your program:

a Add two more mathematics questions to the quiz. You can choose the questions yourself.

b Start the score at 10 instead of 0.

c If the score reaches 14, the Jaime Sprite should say, "You win!" and then end the quiz game by stopping all scripts.

Did you know?

A program that meets all its criteria may still fail if it contains errors that affect how the program runs.

The Mariner 1 Spacecraft in 1962 had a famous software error. A hyphen was omitted in a line of code, which meant that incorrect directions were sent to the spacecraft. The overall cost of the error was reported to be more than $18 million at the time.

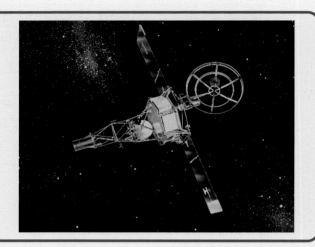

What can you do?

Read and review what you can do.

✔ I can use addition and subtraction in algorithms.

✔ I can develop programs with a variable changed using arithmetic operators.

✔ I can evaluate programs against given criteria.

Great! Now, you can develop algorithms and programs with arithmetic operators in Scratch.

Control systems

Get started!

Do you remember that the simplest form of a control system requires:

- an input device to record data
- a processor to do something with the data
- an output device which the processor instructs?

Work in pairs to answer the following questions:

1 Name the devices shown in A and B. They can be found in the home.
2 How does control system B know what to do?
3 What happens when control system B has completed its task?
4 How does control system A avoid bumping into things?
5 Are control systems found anywhere else, other than homes? If they are, give one example.

You will learn:
- to describe the input-process-output model
- to describe input and output devices that are connected to the internet
- about Artificial Intelligence (AI)
- that AI is used within common software.

Warm up

Work in pairs.

Discuss the following questions based on the weather chart below with your partner.

Sunday	Monday	Tuesday	Wednesday	Thursday	Friday	Saturday
Sunny	Sunny	Partially cloudy	Partially cloudy	Cloudy	Rain clouds	

1 What is the weather on Sunday and Monday?

2 Describe the difference in clouds on Thursday and Friday.

3 a Can you guess what the weather could be on Saturday? Give a reason for your answer.

   b Do you think data gathered by a weather station data logger would help your prediction? Give a reason for your answer.

Share your answers with the class.

Do you remember?

Before you start this unit, check that you know:

- examples where a control system is used
- a range of data recorded by input devices in computer systems, including data that is collected through sensors and data loggers
- a range of manual and automatic input devices
- that computers can be programmed to control machines and other physical objects
- common 'Internet of Things' devices in a familiar environment
- tasks that computers can complete more effectively than humans.

Input-process-output model

The **input-process-output model** helps us understand how a system or process works.

The input-process-output model can be summarised as shown in the following diagram.

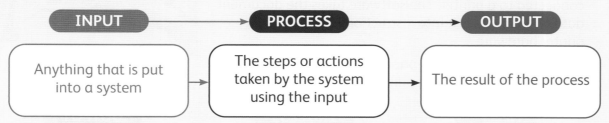

INPUT	PROCESS	OUTPUT
Anything that is put into a system	The steps or actions taken by the system using the input	The result of the process

In computer systems:

- the input is data. Data can be entered manually by humans or automatically by sensors.
- data is processed based on the instructions in a program.
- processed data can be output in many different ways, for example, displayed on the screen, printed on paper, heard as sounds from speakers, and so on.

The input-process-output model can be illustrated with examples relating to different computing devices.

Input-process-output model for a control system

An automatic toaster is a simple control system found in the home. Its input, process and output are:

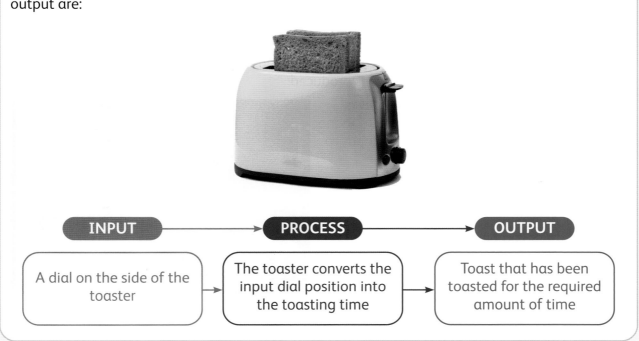

INPUT	PROCESS	OUTPUT
A dial on the side of the toaster	The toaster converts the input dial position into the toasting time	Toast that has been toasted for the required amount of time

Input-process-output model for printing

Printing a document from a computer takes place as follows:

- The data that makes up the document is the input.

- The document data is sent to special printer software. The printer software is installed on any computer connected to a printer. The software takes the document data and processes it into instructions for the printer hardware.

- The printer applies ink on paper so that the document is recreated. The output is a printed copy of the document.

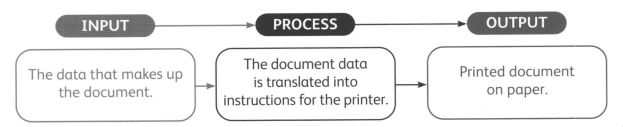

INPUT	PROCESS	OUTPUT
The data that makes up the document.	The document data is translated into instructions for the printer.	Printed document on paper.

Input-process-output model for audio production

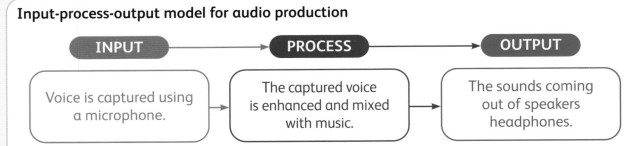

INPUT	PROCESS	OUTPUT
Voice is captured using a microphone.	The captured voice is enhanced and mixed with music.	The sounds coming out of speakers headphones.

Audio production means capturing and enhancing sounds to create an audio product like a song. This example explains how a song is produced:

- A microphone is used as the input device. It captures a singer's voice. The microphone produces electrical signals that are input to a computer.

- Software in the computer processes electrical signals and changes them into digital data. This software can also change this data or combine it with other data to create a song.

- The digital data is turned back into an electrical signal, which drives a speaker. The output is the sound heard through the speakers or headphones.

Practise

1 State whether the following statements are true or false.
   a In computer systems, the input is data.
   b Data can only be entered manually.
   c A sound from a computer speaker is one type of data output.
   d Printing is possible without a printer.
   e A microphone is an input in audio production.

2 Copy the sentences and fill in the blanks using the correct words in the word bank below.

   (output) (hardware) (input) (instructs) (software)

   When any digital file is sent to print, it is sent to special printer _____. This _____ _____ the printer what to do. Finally, the _____ is the printed copy of the file on paper.

3 Work with a partner to answer the following:
   a Describe the input-process-output model for a microwave.
   b Name another control system that can be found in a home.
   c Describe the input-process-output model for the control system identified in part **b** above.

Internet of Things: Inputs and outputs

Learn

You may recall that many everyday devices can connect and interact over the internet. This is called the Internet of Things. Such devices are called smart devices.

Smart devices can be found all around us. There are smart devices in the home. There are smart personal devices that we can wear. There are also smart devices in factories and installed in cities.

Experts estimate that the number of smart devices used in 2010 was just about 1 billion. In 2020, it was almost 12 billion. By 2030, predictions are that up to 30 billion smart devices could be connected to the internet!

Data input

Smart devices can send input data over the internet. They often contain sensors to collect data about their physical environment. This data is then sent over the internet.

A motion detector is used in **smart security systems**. When movement is detected, a light or camera is turned on and starts recording. This footage can be seen by someone connected to the internet.

A motion detector is used in **smart energy systems** in offices. Lights automatically turn on and off as someone enters and exits a room. The lights can send information about when they are on over the internet.

Smart street lights in cities can automatically adjust brightness as they detect the motion of a car or pedestrian. The smart system allows city planners to see when and where energy is being used.

A **smart doorbell** captures video and audio data and alerts a homeowner when someone is at their door. They allow the homeowner to talk to the visitor over the internet.

Smart weather data loggers use sensors to collect data to report and forecast weather. This data includes temperatures, humidity, wind speed and air pressure. All the captured data from multiple smart weather data loggers can be sent over the internet to a central computer. It analyses the data and makes weather predictions in real time.

Smart moisture sensors are used in farms and the food industry, to monitor soil moisture and the condition of stored food.

Getting water into people's homes needs millions of kilometres of pipes. Modern pipe systems use smart moisture sensors to detect leaks and send alerts over the internet to the water company. This stops waste and prevents damage.

Smart thermostats are used to control smart appliances such as air conditioner units, boilers, heaters and radiators.

Smart thermostats monitor and control the temperature of each room at home or office via the internet. Many of them are even voice-controlled through their connectivity with voice assistants such as Siri® and Alexa.

A **smart smoke alarm** notifies users of its battery-life status and when it needs servicing. They can also alert users even when they are away from home.

Outputs

Some IoT devices can produce an output. In an IoT device, a signal is sent over the internet to an **actuator** to produce a physical action or motion. Many of the smart devices mentioned in the data input section also work together with smart actuators.

For example, in smart devices that control lights, there is an actuator mechanism that can turn the light on and off and even change the brightness of the light remotely over the internet.

Devices that monitor moisture can be connected to smart sprinkler systems. The system has an actuator controlled over the internet to turn the water on and off to give plants the correct amount of water.

Smart valve actuators are also used in many industries to control the flow of liquids and gases in pipes. They can shut off or redirect the flow of liquids and gases as needed.

Smart locks used in homes, offices and factories use actuators controlled by an app on a mobile device to lock and unlock doors remotely.

In the manufacturing and medical industries, smart actuators can control the movements of a smart robotic arm that is connected to the internet. This can be used for various tasks, such as lifting a large object in a factory or performing surgery in a hospital.

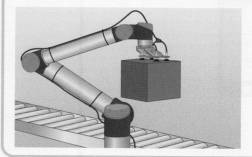

> **Keyword**
>
> **actuator:** a device that can produce movement

Practise

Select the best answer from the options provided for each question below.

1 IoT is short for _____
   a Input output Things
   b Input of Things
   c Internet of Things

2 Which of the following is NOT one of the three main parts of a smart device?
   a actuator
   b internet
   c sensor

3 A sensor is the data _____ for a smart device.
   a control
   b input
   c output

4 An actuator is part of a smart device that _____.
   a analyses the data received
   b detects changes in the environment
   c makes something happen

5 Which of the following sensors will detect changes in the brightness around?
   a acoustic sensor
   b image sensor
   c light sensor

6 Which actuator is used to assist in surgeries?
   a smart valve
   b smart robotic arm
   c smart sprinkler

7 Which actuator is used to prevent explosions in a factory with gases in their pipes?
   a smart valve
   b smart robotic arm
   c smart sprinkler

Artificial Intelligence

Human beings are called intelligent because we can continuously learn new things and solve problems.

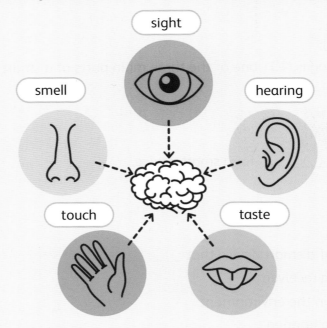

Many computer systems cannot function without a human being to control them.

For example:

- Humans can control these systems using input devices – for example, you might control a robot with a joystick.
- Humans can control these systems by programming them to follow exact instructions – for example, you might program a robot to take a path through a maze.

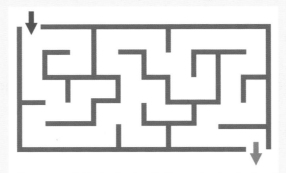

These computer systems do not display intelligence. They do not learn and they do not solve problems.

However, other computer systems do have the ability to learn and problem-solve. For instance, some robots can find their own way out of a maze.

All machines and computers are called artificial because they are not 'natural' – they are made by humans.

Artificial Intelligence (AI) is the ability of a machine or computer to think and act on its own to accomplish a task, like a human.

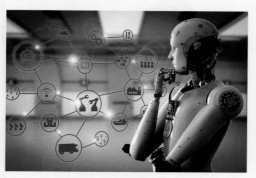

> **Keywords**
>
> **joystick:** an input device that can be used to control movement in several directions
>
> **Artificial Intelligence:** when a computer system or machine appears to think and act like a human on its own
>
> **autonomous:** can function on its own

AI is a simulation of human intelligence. This means it can look much like human intelligence.

Some common computer systems use Artificial Intelligence. You may have used AI without realising it.

Online video websites use AI to recommend videos for you to watch. The AI learns what videos you like and what topics you are interested in. Over time it becomes better at recommending.

Many computer devices use AI for facial recognition, to allow access to the device. The AI recognises your face before letting you onto your device.

AI allows autonomous vehicles to work. For instance, an AI can learn how to drive. It learns to steer along a road and to recognise potential dangers. Once it has learnt, it can drive safely on roads it has never been on before.

Some software on computers also uses AI to make it easier and faster for humans to write text. AI can speed up the process using **predictive text** and **speech-to-text**.

Predictive text

Some devices or software suggest words and phrases to complete your sentence. This feature is known as predictive text.

Predictive text works by creating a personalised dictionary of words and phrases for each user. It learns how words are used together and how often they are used. The more often a word or phrase is used, the more likely that word will be suggested.

The AI can even predict names and slang phrases.

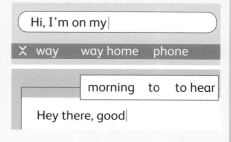

Speech-to-text

A speech-to-text AI can convert spoken words into text on the screen without the need for a keyboard.

A microphone is used as the input device.

This feature is useful if someone is unable to type using a keyboard. It can also speed up writing.

Because each person has a unique accent and way of speaking, the AI needs to be 'trained'. To do this, the user reads out some text provided by the software. This lets the AI learn how the user pronounces these words.

The AI continues to learn every time the user corrects it. This increases the accuracy of the AI over time.

Practise

1 State whether the following statements are true or false.
   a All computer systems are artificial.
   b AI means 'after input'.
   c Facial recognition is not an example of Artificial Intelligence.
   d Autonomous vehicles need a driver to detect and prevent an accident.
   e The more a word is used, the more likely it is to be suggested by the predictive text.
   f Predictive text can speed up typing a letter.
   g Slang phrases cannot be added to predictive text.
   h A microphone is needed for speech-to-text.
   i Speech-to-text is useful if a person is unable to type.
   j A speech-to-text AI needs to be trained.

2 Copy the sentences and fill in the blanks using the words in the word bank below.

   (predictive) (faster) (intelligence) (speech) (keyboard)

   In the past, typing a letter in a word processor would depend solely on the input of the person typing on a _____. Now, some software on computers uses AI to make it easier and _____ for humans to write. Artificial _____ can help speed up the typing process with features like; ' _____ text' and ' _____ -to-text'.

Go further

1   Draw a line to match the labels to the descriptions.

   INPUT   The steps or actions taken by the system, using the input

   PROCESS   Different ways a system presents the results after processing

   OUTPUT   Whatever is put into a system

2   Work with a partner to complete the following task.
   a   What is the input for a smart smoke alarm system?
   b   What type of actuator will a smart fire sprinkler system use to turn on the water when the system detects a fire?
   c   Name two other places the same type of actuator that is identified in **b** above is used.

3   Work with a partner to complete the following task.
   a   Name two-word processor features that use Artificial Intelligence.
   b   Give one benefit for each of the two features named in part **a**.

Challenge yourself!

1   Work with a partner to fill in the blanks using the words in the word bank below.

   (systems)   (fixing)   (input)   (understand)   (output)   (processes)

   The _____-process-_____ model is commonly used to describe many _____ and _____.
   It can be used to help better _____ how systems work. It can also assist in identifying
   issues and _____ them if a system does not function as it should.

2   Draw a line to match the actuators to their uses.

   Smart lock   Controls smart sprinkler system

   Robotic arm   Secures hotel doors

   Smart valve   Assists in surgeries

3   Work with a partner to complete the following task.
   a   Explain to your partner how predictive text works in word processor software.
   b   Let your partner explain to you how speech-to-text works in word processor software.

157

My project

Work in groups of 3–4 to complete the following task:

1   Pia is designing an autonomous vehicle that does not need a driver to detect and avoid bumping into things. Help Pia research and design a plan for a model autonomous car.

a   Draw a simple diagram to show and describe the input-process-output model for the model car.

b   What type of IoT input devices will be the best choice for the car? Give a reason for the type of IoT input chosen.

c   i   What is an actuator?

   ii   What would an IoT actuator do on your car to help steer it? Give a reason for your answer.

d   An autonomous vehicle uses AI to help detect and avoid bumping into things.

   i   What do the letters 'AI' stand for?

   ii   List two types of AI features found in productivity software, such as in a word processor. Explain how these two AI features work and what their benefits are.

What can you do?

Read and review what you can do.

✔ I know about the input-process-output model.

✔ I can talk about computing devices and mechanisms that are connected to the internet.

✔ I know that Artificial Intelligence (AI) is a simulation of human intelligence within computer systems.

✔ I know that AI is used in predictive text and speech-to-text.

Problem solving

Get started!

In groups of three, discuss which of the following are inputs and outputs of a micro:bit.

a Buttons

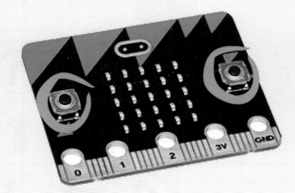

b LED (lights)

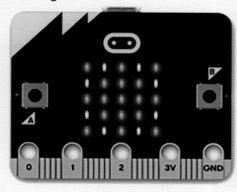

c Sound

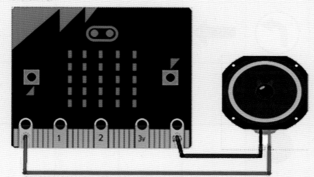

d Touch sensor (logo)

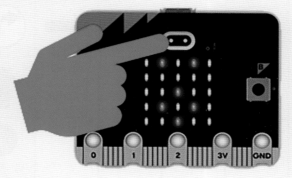

You will learn:

• that some algorithms are more efficient than others

• to develop programs with 'equal to' comparison operators

• to develop programs for the micro:bit using selection to produce different outputs.

In this unit, you will develop algorithms and programs using MakeCode for micro:bit.

Warm up

Look at the two paths that these robot vacuum cleaners take to reach the exit.

It takes each robot 1 second to move one block forward and 2 seconds to make a right or left turn.

Work in pairs. Which robot's path is more efficient, A or B?

Hint: The robot that takes the shortest time is more efficient.

↱	→	→	→	EXIT	←	←	←	↰
↑								↑
↑						↱	→	↴
↳	←	←	←	↰	↱	→	↴	
				↑	↑			
				⚫ A	⚫ B			

Do you remember?

Before starting this unit, check that you:

- can use selection in algorithms such as IF, THEN, ELSE statements
- can use comparison (equal to) operators in algorithms
- can develop programs with a variable assigned to a specific value.

In this unit, you will use MakeCode for micro:bit.

There is an online chapter all about MakeCode for micro:bit.

Algorithm to code
Efficient algorithms

Learn

Different algorithms may complete the same task with a different set of instructions. The most efficient algorithm is the one that:

- takes the least amount of time to run or
- uses the least number of steps.

When creating an algorithm, you should break problems down and put the parts together in the correct way to create the solution.

Comparison of algorithms

Recall the two robots' paths from the **Warm-up** activity. Paths A and B both get the robot to the exit.

Look at the two algorithms below. These two algorithms represent Paths A and B. They both solve the same problem.

Algorithm A	
①	Move forward 2 blocks
②	Turn 90 degrees left
③	Move forward 4 blocks
④	Turn 90 degrees right
⑤	Move forward 3 blocks
⑥	Turn 90 degrees right
⑦	Move forward 4 blocks

Algorithm B	
①	Move forward 2 blocks
②	Turn 90 degrees right
③	Move forward 2 blocks
④	Turn 90 degrees left
⑤	Move forward 1 block
⑥	Turn 90 degrees right
⑦	Move forward 2 blocks
⑧	Turn 90 degrees left
⑨	Move forward 2 blocks
⑩	Turn 90 degrees left
⑪	Move forward 4 blocks

Algorithm A is more efficient!

Algorithm A is more efficient than Algorithm B at completing the task.

- There are fewer steps in Algorithm A, so it takes less time to process.
- There are more left/right turns in Algorithm B. It takes longer to complete Path B as turns take 2 seconds and forward movements take 1 second.

Practise

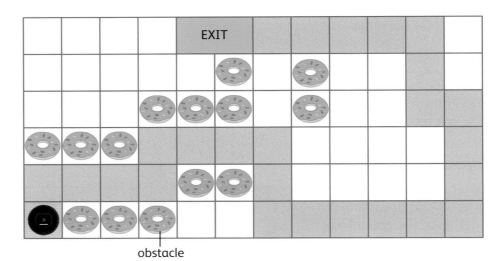

obstacle

1 Look at Algorithm A below for another robot vacuum cleaner to reach the exit. There is a quicker path that the robot can take. The robot should avoid all obstacles. Re-write the algorithm to be more efficient. Complete the table on the right.

Algorithm A	
①	Move forward 1 block
②	Turn 90 degrees right
③	Move forward 3 blocks
④	Turn 90 degrees left
⑤	Move forward 1 block
⑥	Turn 90 degrees right
⑦	Move forward 3 blocks
⑧	Turn 90 degrees right
⑨	Move forward 2 blocks
⑩	Turn 90 degrees left
⑪	Move forward 5 blocks
⑫	Turn 90 degrees left
⑬	Move forward 3 blocks
⑭	Turn 90 degrees left
⑮	Move forward 1 block
⑯	Turn 90 degrees right
⑰	Move forward 2 blocks
⑱	Turn 90 degrees left
⑲	Move forward 5 blocks

Algorithm B	
①	
②	
③	
④	
⑤	
⑥	
⑦	
⑧	
⑨	
⑩	
⑪	

Compare your answer with your partner's.

2 Describe in your own words what an efficient algorithm is.

Comparison operators

Learn

You should recall how to create algorithms and programs with an 'equal to' operator. Remember that 'equal to' is an example of a comparison operator.

In this section, we will create a program using MakeCode for micro:bit with an 'equal to' operator and the conditional 'If …Then …' statement.

We will create a **Rock, Paper, Scissors** game. In this example, we will create part of the program. The code should match the algorithm below.

Part 1 of algorithm	
①	Start program when micro:bit is shaken
②	Create variable called Hand
③	Choose a random number from 1 to 3
④	Set variable Hand to value in Step 3
⑤	**5.1** If variable Hand = 1, then **5.1.1** Show LEDs of rock icon

Recall the **If…Then** … coding block only runs the instructions inside the block if the condition is true. In the code below, only if the value is 1, will the micro:bit display a rock icon.

Program with 'equal to' operator

In this program, when the micro:bit is shaken, it selects a random number from 1 to 3. If the number is 1, the micro:bit will show a rock icon on its LED display. The code that matches the algorithm is shown.

In this program, we used the **pick random** coding block and entered the values 1 and 3 for the range of numbers to be selected. The variable **Hand** is set to store the value of the number that is randomly chosen.

The **equal to** coding block inside the **If … Then …** coding block compares the value of the variable **Hand** to the number 1. If Hand stored the number 1, then the condition is true and the **show leds** block runs.

If Hand stored the numbers 2 or 3, then the condition is not true and the **show leds** block does not run.

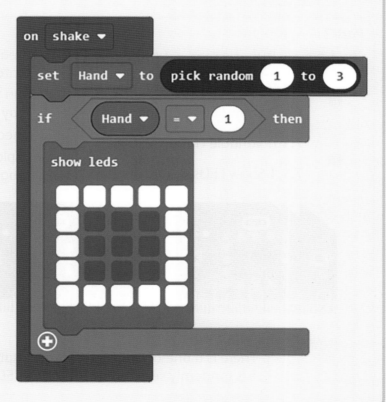

163

Practise

Part 1

We will create the program on the last page using MakeCode for micro:bit.

1   Open a new project.
2   Add the blocks of code shown on the last page.
   ● Create a variable called **Hand** by selecting the **Variables** group of blocks, then click **Make a Variable**, type the name of the variable and click **OK**.
   ● Find the **Set to** and variable **Hand** coding blocks from **Variables** group of blocks.
   ● Find the **Pick random** block from the **Math** group.
   ● Find the **If** and **Equal to** blocks from the **Logic** group.

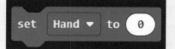 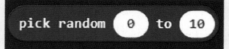 

3   Click the **Play** button on the left of the screen to start the simulator and click the **shake** button to test your code.

If using the physical device, you should follow the additional instructions on using the physical micro:bit for running a program.

Part 2

Part 2 (algorithm continued from part 1)	
6	**6.1** If variable Hand = 2, then
	6.1.1 Show LEDs of paper icon
7	**7.1** If variable Hand = 2, then
	7.1.1 Show LEDs of scissors icon

1   Create the final part of the program to match the algorithm below.
2   Run your program by clicking the **Play** button.
3   Check that you get the correct results.
4   Explain to your partner what this program does.

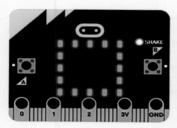 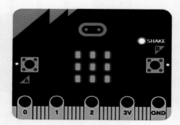 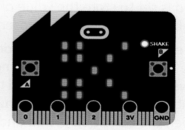

There is a one-out-of-three chance that the number 1 is randomly selected and that the LEDs light.

Conditional statements

Learn

You should recall from previous units what conditional statements are.

In the previous section, we used the **If … Then …** conditional statement. In this section, we will develop programs for the micro:bit using **If … Then … Else** statements to produce different outputs.

Example of a program with If … Then … Else

In this example, we will create a flashlight on the micro:bit. When Button A is pressed, all the LEDs on the micro:bit should light. Otherwise, all the LEDs should remain off.

First, we create an algorithm to meet these requirements.

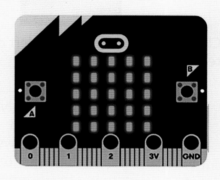

Algorithm A	
①	Start program when Play button is pressed
②	**2.1** If Button A is pressed, then **2.1.1** Show all LEDs **2.2** Else **2.2.1** Clear LED screen
③	Repeat step 2 forever

With **If … Then … Else** statements, there will be two possible outputs: one if the condition is true and one if it is false.

The code as shown matches each line in the algorithm.

This program for the micro:bit produces two different outputs based on a condition being true or false.

You need to hold button A down to keep the 'torch' on.

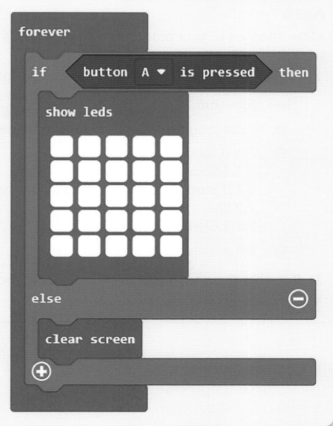

Practise

Part A

Create the program for the micro:bit from the **Learn** panel as follows:

1 Open a new project on MakeCode for micro:bit.

2 Add all the code on the previous page to the programming area.

- Find the **If … Then … Else** coding block from the **Logic** group of blocks.
- Find the **Button A is pressed** coding block from the **Input** group.
- Find the **Clear screen** block from the **Basic** group of blocks.

3 Click the **Play** button on the left of the screen to start the simulator and click **Button A** to test your code.

If using the physical device, you should follow the additional instructions on using the physical micro:bit for running a program.

Do you get the required results when you run your program?

Part B

Make changes to your program to light the LEDs and play a melody if the logo (touch sensor) is pressed as follows.

1 Add/change your code to match this new algorithm in the table below.

New algorithm	
❶	Start program when Play button is pressed
❷	**2.1** If logo is pressed, then **2.1.1** Show all LEDs **2.1.2** Start dadadum melody repeating once **2.2** Else **2.2.1** Clear LED screen
❸	Repeat step 2 forever

2 Run your program and check that you get the desired results.

3 Compare your solution with your partner.

Go further

Computational thinking

Which algorithm below is more efficient to display the letter 'i' on the micro:bit? Explain why.

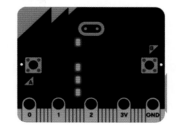

Algorithm A

❶	Start program when Play button is pressed
❷	Plot x(1), y(4)
❸	Plot x(1), y(3)
❹	Plot x(1), y(2)
❺	Plot x(1), y(0)

Algorithm B

❶	Start program when Play button is pressed
❷	Show string 'i'

Lisa wants to check how many steps she walks around her house. Help Lisa create a step counter on the micro:bit.

1   Open a new project.

2   Create a program that counts by clicking a button. Your code should match the algorithm in the table below.

Step	Instruction
❶	Start program when Play button is pressed
❷	Create variable called Step
❸	Set variable Step to 0
❹	**4.1** If Button A is pressed, then: **4.1.1** Change variable Step by 1 **4.1.2** Show number of variable Step **4.2** Else **4.2.1** Clear LED screen
❺	Repeat step 4 forever

Compare your code with your partner's.

3   What instructions should be added if Lisa wanted the micro:bit to play a spring sound if the number of steps reaches 10?

Make these changes to your code.

4   Test your code and check that you get the required results.

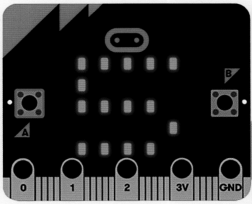

⭐ **Challenge yourself!**

We will create a new program for the micro:bit that reads the light level (level of light present).

1 Open a new project in MakeCode for micro:bit.

2 Add the code shown below to your project.

   • Create a variable called **reading**.

   • Find the **light level** coding block from the **Input** group of blocks.

   • Find the **plot bar graph** coding block from **Led** group of blocks.

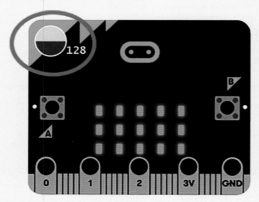

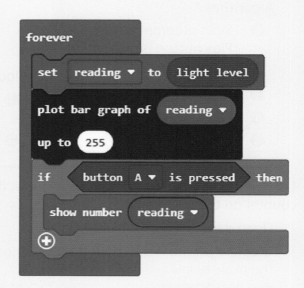

The **light level** coding block uses the light sensor. The light sensor on the micro:bit can detect how light it is. The light level is measured on a scale from 0 to 255, so the bar graph reading is from 0 to 255.

3 Run and test your code. Determine how this program works.

4 In the simulator, you can change the light level. What happens on the LED display when the simulated light level is **a)** 255 **b)** 0?

5 Write an algorithm that matches the code above by completing the table shown.

Step	Instruction (New Algorithm)
❶	Start program when _____
❷	Create variable _____
❸	Get light level reading from light sensor
❹	Set _____
❺	Plot bar graph _____
❻	**6.1** If _____ **6.1.1** Show _____
❼	Repeat steps _____

> On the simulator, you can change the amount of light present by changing the amount of yellow in the circle.

My project

Liam needs to create a digital pet for a school project. Help Liam do this by creating a pet hamster on the micro:bit.

1   If we wanted the hamster's eyes to blink, which algorithm below would be more efficient?

Algorithm A	
❶	Start program when Play button is pressed
❷	Show LEDs of eyes icon
❸	Clear LED screen
❹	Show LEDs of eyes icon
❺	Clear LED screen
❻	Repeat steps 2 to 5 forever

Algorithm B	
❶	Start program when Play button is pressed
❷	Plot x(1), y(1)
❸	Plot x(3), y(1)
❹	Pause for 1 second (1000ms)
❺	Plot x(1), y(1)
❻	Plot x(3), y(1)
❼	Pause for 1 second (1000ms)
❽	Repeat steps 2 to 7 forever

Explain the reason for your answer.

2   Create a program for the Hamster to say "hello" as follows:

Compare your program with your partner's.

- Create a variable called **Count** in a new project.
- On start, set Count to 0.
- On logo pressed, change Count by 1.
- If Count is equal to 3, play a hello sound until done.
- Repeat the conditional **If … Then … Else** statement forever so that this condition is always checked.

3   Add code to display the Hamster's happy and sad face as follows:

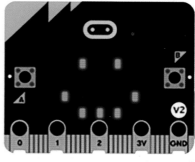

Step	Instruction
❶	Start program when Play button is pressed
❷	**2.1** If Button A is pressed, then: **2.1.1** Show LEDs of happy face icon **2.2** Else: **2.2.1** Clear LED screen
❸	**3.1** If Button B is pressed, then: **3.1.1** Show LEDs of sad face icon **3.2** Else: **3.2.1** Clear LED screen
❹	Repeat steps 2 to 3 forever

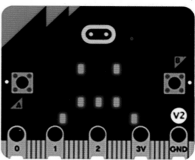

4   Run and test your program to check that you get the correct result. Debug any errors.

Did you know?

Traffic lights are a real-life application of efficient programming.

Traffic lights follow algorithms that move traffic safely but as quickly as possible.

An efficient algorithm can determine the best time to change each traffic light using the fewest steps.

What can you do?

Read and review what you can do.

- ✔ I can identify which algorithms are most efficient.
- ✔ I can develop programs with the 'equal to' comparison operator.
- ✔ I can develop programs for the micro:bit using conditions to produce different outputs.

Great! Now, you can develop algorithms and programs on MakeCode for micro:bit.